# THE PEOPLE OF THE TWILIGHT

Ikpuck and Icehouse.

# THE PEOPLE
# OF THE TWILIGHT

DIAMOND JENNESS

THE UNIVERSITY OF CHICAGO PRESS
CHICAGO & LONDON

*TO MY MOTHER*

International Standard Book Number: 0-226-39653-3

THE UNIVERSITY OF CHICAGO PRESS, CHICAGO 60637
The University of Chicago Press, Ltd., London

# PREFACE

ONE cannot read this charming narrative of the author's life during two years with the primitive Eskimos of the Coronation Gulf Region without getting a deep sympathy for these simple, unsophisticated children of the twilight, who are still living in their communistic state, and have not felt the burden of wealth—except perhaps that someone of their best men, like "Knife," may have so much domestic equipment that it is difficult to pack all his belongings on one dog sledge when they are wandering.

Surely many readers will feel a longing to live in the snow hut or in the tent under the good care of Mother Icehouse, to go stalking the caribou or watch for the seals at their breathing holes with Father Ikpuck and the "Runner," or to play with little bright sister Jenny Sunshine.

A charming people of happy children, not yet stung by the venom of our culture, not burdened by the intricate problems and the acid dissatisfaction of our society. Starving sometimes perhaps when food is scarce (but that does not last long) ; and when food is plentiful life is laughing happiness with no sorrows of the past and none for the morrow. They live happily but under extreme conditions. During ages they have learnt to master the severe forces of nature, and no other people can take their place and develop the possibilities of those northern regions. But contact with our civilization, when not carefully guarded as in Greenland, will upset the whole system of their life and community, and they must sink.

[ v ]

The greedy white men wish to get hold of their furs; but what do we give them instead? Our products, some of which are of very doubtful value to them, indeed, and then our ghastly, insidious diseases, and often our bad customs and morals.

They had fitted their life into the conditions of their surroundings; with their old weapons taxing the game sufficiently to satisfy amply their requirements, without reducing the stock. Then we bring them rifles, nay, even magazine rifles, offering to buy the skins. The slaughter begins; the game, formerly so abundant, will in a few years be more or less exterminated, and the main condition that made their life possible be gone.

What a sad guilt we white men have towards native races! But these people live in a land that will be of no value to us without them.

Let there be no doubt about it; they, too, are doomed if nothing really effective is done to protect them. The land of the great white silence will never more ring with the happy mirth of these lovable children of the twilight.

Surely the Canadian people and authorities will not allow such a thing to happen, when once their attention has been drawn to it. No one can be deaf to the thrilling appeal with which the author ends his book. May he be the harbinger of a brighter dawn in twilight land. The problem must be faced, but at once and with intelligent prudence, unless it shall be too late.

FRIDTJOF NANSEN

Lysaker

# CONTENTS

# THE PEOPLE
## OF THE TWILIGHT

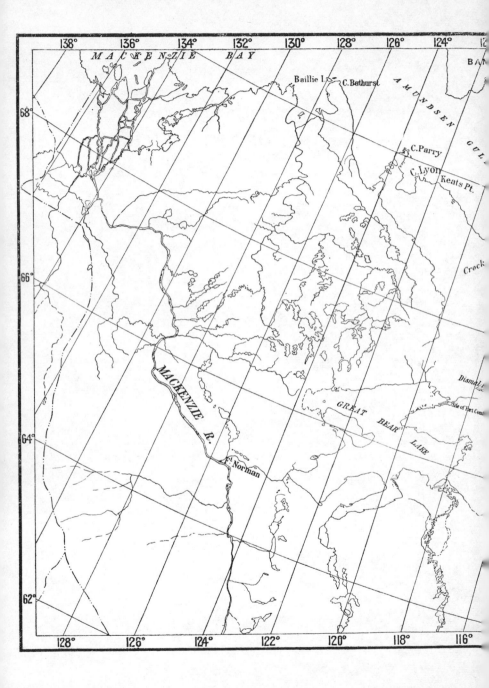

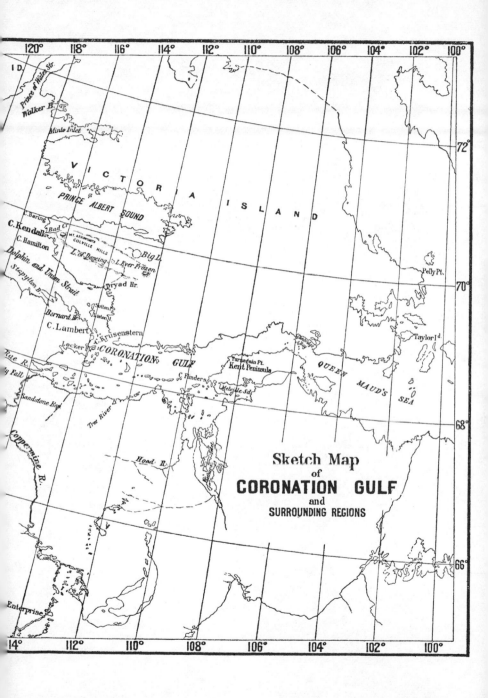

Sketch Map
of
CORONATION GULF
and
SURROUNDING REGIONS

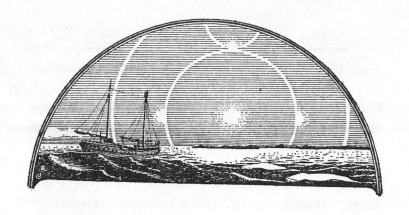

# CHAPTER I

## THE PROMISED LAND

A THICK fog had settled down upon the *North Star,* shutting everything from view save the big grounded ice-cake to which the schooner was moored. Now and then a momentary rift revealed a flat, gravelly beach two hundred yards to the south, and a moss-covered land sloping gently back to an interior plateau in a series of low terraces separated by innumerable ponds. All about us the sea was covered with a maze of floating ice which had gathered into a solid mass around a low cape half a mile to the eastward. We had run into a small bay, that was certain; and Bernard Harbour, the haven of our voyage, was not more than a few miles away. Beyond that we knew nothing. Even if no fog had held us up we should have been no wiser, for the admiralty chart of this region, based on voyages of nearly a century before, was none too accurate. All we could do for the present was to tie up until the weather cleared and made it safe to venture once more among the floes.

My watch came in the early hours of the morning. It was the end of August, and the nights were still short, although the sun no longer circled around the sky throughout the whole twenty-four hours of the day. The Aurora Borealis was staging its last performance as I stepped on deck. Right across the northern sky stretched a giant arc bright with all the colours of the rainbow, and beneath flickered two filmy curtains of white light faintly tinged with rose. They lasted only a moment, then changed into a dazzling, whirling eddy that sent out flashing streamers, red and white and gold, that vanished as quickly as they appeared. Finally the eddy faded also, and a pale grey hue suffusing the eastern sky ushered in the dawn.

I sat down in the stern to meditate. It was ten days since we had said farewell to the friendly post of the Mounted Police at Herschel Island, turned our backs on the last outpost of civilization, and steered the *North Star* eastward. We had sailed over 500 miles in those ten days, and slept little, for the season was far advanced, and the ice, if it closed in at any time, might prevent our reaching the tiny bay in Dolphin and Union Strait which we had chosen for our winter quarters. Often I had peered down from the wheel into the smoky engine-room where Cox, our topographer, crouched wearily over the engine, hour after hour, as if the fate of the whole expedition depended on his wakefulness. When the sea was free from ice and the engine running smoothly, he would sometimes lie down to sleep for a few minutes, or, half fainting, stagger up the ladder to fill his lungs with a few mouthfuls of sweet, fresh air before returning to his self-imposed duty. Castel and myself, who took turns at the wheel, were almost equally exhausted; yet day and night we had kept on our course. Now the voyage was nearly ended; a few hours of calm, clear weather should enable us to find the harbour, where our second schooner, the *Alaska,* had doubtless cast anchor already and landed the rest of our party.

A soft splash in the water roused me from these meditations. Looking up, I saw a small hair seal raise its head above the surface not forty yards away. It dived before I could seize my rifle, but appeared again nearer the vessel a few minutes later. The shot went true, and, with the assistance of Cox, who appeared on deck immediately, I was about to lower the canoe to drag in the carcass when two more shots echoed faintly across the water from the eastward. We fired again, and again we heard the answer; so, picking up the seal, we raised anchor and steamed outward, hugging the shore and sounding at intervals with the lead. The fog had lifted a little and, as we rounded a low point, we sighted a canoe coming toward us with Anderson, our commander, paddling in the bow. Beyond, at the end of a narrow bay, the *Alaska* was anchored close to the beach, and two large tents gleamed white in the misty sunlight. Here at last was our harbour. But the channel up which we were heading contained hardly enough water to float the canoe in which Anderson had come to meet us. The real entrance was a bottle-shaped gap beyond the low island on our left. We turned the ship about and ran down to it, only to find it blocked by heavy ice-floes. So once again we curbed our impatience and anchored under the lee of a small reef until either the tide or the wind should open up a passage.

The fog was denser than ever the next morning, but the sea calm and unruffled. After a hasty breakfast we weighed anchor, and, running down to the barrier of floes, tried to force our way through. We charged it at full speed, and nosed the vessel's prow into the opening cracks; or we backed out and charged again, twisting this way and that wherever a dark streak of water marked the end of one floe and the beginning of another. Sometimes the bow of the *North Star* climbed right on top of a floe; but we clambered onto the ice, and pushed her off again with poles. Yard by yard we worked our way forward until, just before noon, we squeezed through the last two floes that blocked the passage and dropped anchor beside the *Alaska*. The long voyage was ended; after fifteen months of wandering we had reached our goal at last.

# CHAPTER II

## AN OUTPOST ON THE POLAR SEA

IN the summer of 1912 a pioneer trader cruising
along the Arctic coast of Canada discovered,
behind a low island, a tiny deep-water cove,
afterward named in his honour Bernard Harbour. The
cove is now the regional headquarters of three distinct
organizations—the Hudson's Bay Company, the
Anglican Mission, and the Royal Canadian Mounted
Police; but when the *Alaska* and the *North Star* sailed
into it, in August, 1914, the country was still bare
and seemingly uninhabited. Low, stony ridges,
sparsely covered with mosses and lichens, concealed
all the region to the south and west, and across the
narrow neck of land that bounded the cove on its
eastern side was a second inlet similar to our own,
but less sheltered from the prevailing winds. On this
narrow neck of land we decided to set up our station.

We spent two busy days unloading our cargoes
onto the beach. A propeller blade of the *Alaska* had
been broken against an ice-cake, and the engineer had

to replace it with another before she could return to Herschel Island for our yearly mail and the remainder of our supplies. He accomplished the work without difficulty, and the schooner left a few days later with Anderson in charge. We expected her to rejoin us before the sea froze over for the winter, but on her return voyage she encountered a heavy gale and an unprecedented rise of the tide at Cape Bathurst, 300 miles west of Bernard Harbour. Tide and gale left her high and dry on the beach, and by the time she was unloaded and refloated the season had grown too late for her to venture out again. Anderson himself travelled along the coast with a dog-team and rejoined us in midwinter; but throughout the autumn there were only five white men and one Eskimo at Bernard Harbour to construct a station and carry on the scientific work.

Chipman, the senior topographer, was in charge of the party, but so smoothly and tactfully did he rule that no one felt his guiding hand. We allowed Palaiyak, our Eskimo, to devote his whole time to hunting seals and caribou. The rest of us took turns at the cooking, our official cook having gone west on the *Alaska*. Scientists are not always successful in the kitchen. I myself was very partial to boiled rice, one of the few dishes I could undertake with certainty; but since plain, unadorned rice, and even rice with raisins in it, seemed to be unpopular with the other

[ 7 ]

men, I improvised extra meals of powerful doughnuts to dull the edges of their appetites. Chipman, O'Neill, the geologist, and Johansen, the biologist, always provided good fare, although Johansen's enthusiasm for pure science often restricted us to two meals a day. But it was for Cox, the junior topographer, that we reserved our greatest respect. He startled us one day by placing on the table a splendid cake covered with rich chocolate icing. Our eyes gleamed with anticipation; it was the first real cake we had seen for many months, and each man grabbed simultaneously for the dish. O'Neill won; two quick cuts of the knife landed a huge slice in front of him. Then a roar of laughter shook the room, for the body of the cake was solid cold cornmeal mush left over from our breakfast.

Our first task after the *Alaska* left was to erect a house for the approaching winter. September with its shortening days had come upon us, and snow might fall at any time, snow that would not disappear before the following June. Building in the Arctic is by no means as difficult as in the Antarctic. There is little or no vegetation in the latter region, and in consequence no soil, so that a winter house offers no comfort unless it has double or triple walls of close-fitting boards lined with tar paper, felt, or other non-conducting material. But the tundrous soil of the Arctic provides the finest kind of sheathing for a house. All that is needed is a wooden framework strong enough to support a layer of turf fifteen or eighteen inches thick around the walls and two or three inches thick on the roof. Once the snow drifts over such a dwelling a room large enough to shelter several men can be made unbearably hot with a small wood-burning stove, even though there are two or three windows in the sides and a ventilator in the ceiling.

Our plans called for a one-roomed hut eighteen by twelve feet, oriented east and west, with a large three-paned window on the south face and a smaller two-paned window on the north. We had brought from Alaska 1,000 feet of roughly dressed lumber; for although the coast east and west of the delta of the Mackenzie River is strewn with driftwood for three or four hundred miles, hardly a single log can be found around Coronation Gulf, none of its rivers reaching back to the heavy forests. Some of us sorted out the lumber and dug post-holes; others cut squares of turf from a neighbouring meadow and transported them to the house-site on a dog-sled. We completed the framework in three days. Each man then undertook to construct one section of the outer wall of turf. Chipman laboured incessantly, as befitted the leader, and the wall in his section mounted rapidly toward the eave; but it suddenly collapsed when it reached two-thirds of its height, compelling him to begin over again from a wider base. None of us were carpenters by trade, and we worked to a large extent indepen-

dently of one another. Consequently the hut developed
a queer twist forward, and the wall sagged in the middle of one side through the weight of an enormously
thick rampart of turf. A building inspector would have
condemned the structure in unequivocal terms, and
ordered its immediate demolition; but we cheerfully
removed the superfluous turf and added a few supports
in the weaker places to prevent our own destruction.
We then built a large porch at the eastern end to protect the door, and roofed it with a heavy tarpaulin.
Last of all we lined the inner walls with white canvas,
and fitted bunks around three sides, one for each member of the party.

Thus our rude hut encased in earth became the
cosiest dwelling within 500 miles. For two long years
we fondly called it "home," and on occasions of state
hoisted the Canadian flag. The banner was changed
after our return to civilization, the hut becoming the
headquarters of an Anglican mission; but even today,
twelve years after its erection, the frame stands perfect, a lasting monument to the skill and ingenuity of
its builders.

After the building of the house came the construction of caches. Most of the larger cases containing
cereals, hardtack, and other foods had gone to make
the porch, which served on occasion also as a meat-
cache. The ammunition, sacks of flour, and various
boxes of miscellaneous provisions were piled in three

heaps and covered with heavy tarpaulins. A single large tent protected the travelling equipment, the bales of skins and spare clothing, and the scientific instruments. We stacked the distillate for the engines on the beach just above high-water level, and laid beside it two large tanks, thinking they held alcohol for scientific specimens. Only one tank was required during the two years we spent in the country. We broached the second just before leaving, and found that it contained, not the alcohol we were expecting, but tooth-brushes, tooth-paste, and shaving-soap, those indispensable articles of toilet of which we had almost forgotten the names.

The construction of caches by no means ended the work around the station; we had still to gather drift-wood from the neighbouring beaches for our winter fuel. Fortunately we could combine this task with scientific work. When Johansen and O'Neill went out to collect insects, plants and fossils along the coast, they made piles of all the logs they discovered in their wanderings; and when Chipman and Cox sounded out the channels leading into our harbour they brought back in their launch several cords of wood gathered on the islands lying off shore. Sleds and dog-teams replaced the launch as soon as the sea froze over, and a wood-gathering party sallied out once a week all through the autumn and winter months.

At the end of the harbour we set a large fish-net,

which was inspected every second day. It yielded at first a few salmon-trout weighing from seven to ten pounds, but when the fall came, nothing but sculpins, a small fish reputed to have a very delicate flavour. It may be that this reputation properly attaches to another species, for all that we captured were so bony that we could never discover any meat. Johansen was pleased with them, however, because they swelled his biological collection beyond all measure; whereas the salmon-trout he had to send into the kitchen after the briefest examination of their colours.

Our main hope for a winter supply of fresh meat rested on the caribou which migrated each spring from the barren grounds to the Arctic coast and the islands that lie north of it. The routes they followed varied from year to year, but we confidently expected that some at least of the numerous herds which pastured on Victoria Island during the summer months would cross the strait in the vicinity of Bernard Harbour on their return migration. Palaiyak, who was an experienced hunter, wandered out in search of them nearly every morning. The large herds never came, although individual caribou and a few small herds of three and four strayed within a radius of ten miles. Of these Palaiyak secured his fair share; but our party of six consumed so much meat that only a little could be stored away for the winter. We discovered afterward that the lateness of the freeze-up had caused the main body of the caribou to migrate along the southern shores of Victoria Island and cross the strait farther to the eastward.

Seals were as valuable to us as caribou, if only to feed the dogs which, like ourselves, preferred a diet of fresh meat to pemmican; consequently the shooting of seals and ptarmigan became our principal recreation at the end of each day's work. It is not easy to hit the small, round head of a seal that appears just above the water-line fifty or eighty yards away and disappears a few seconds later; the chances of success are particularly slim when you are kneeling in the bow of a small Peterborough canoe that bobs up and down with each wave. Yet we shot over a score of seals before the winter closed in, Palaiyak himself killing six in one day. We fed all the meat and blubber to the dogs, retaining the livers for our own table. Fried seal-liver for breakfast, followed by roast ptarmigan at noon, would delight the heart of any epicure. Even the dogs showed their appreciation, for more than once they broke into the meat-cache and cheated us of these hoarded luxuries.

In spite of these varied activities, scientific work was by no means neglected. Chipman and Cox established the latitude and longitude of our station, placed the meteorological instruments in position, and connected the anemometer with a small electric bulb inside the house so that we could ascertain the direction and velocity of the wind by simply moving a switch; the winter before, with a different type of anemometer, we had crouched in the snow outdoors and read a dial on the base of the instrument. We made soundings, too, inside and outside the harbour, and Johansen collected marine specimens in both places, using a drag-net towed behind the launch during the autumn months, and, after the freeze-up, a hand-net let down through holes in the ice. On stormy days we developed photographs and worked up our field-notes of the preceding year.

Sunday was generally a day of rest, given over to reading, long walks, and similar recreations. Saturday evenings we devoted to bridge, a game that was strictly forbidden on other days of the week. As we sat around the card-table one stormy night, Palaiyak reported that the wind was carrying away the tarpaulin that covered the porch. We dropped the cards on the table and rushed to the rescue, not lingering to put on overshoes or heavy clothing. Two men climbed to the roof and held it down with their weight; the others sought around the caches for boulders, bags, and anything else that would serve to batten down the tarpaulin. It was pitch dark, and the snow, driven by the howling gale, lashed our faces like hail. Cox, carrying a huge block of ice in his arms, crashed into Chipman, who was packing a sack of coal. Fingers and toes began to freeze, and excitement ran high for a few minutes. But gradually the tarpaulin ceased to flap, the men on the roof came down from their perches, and we mustered around the warm stove again to thaw out our members and count the casualties.

The expedition fad four dog-teams, each at daggers drawn with the rest so that we chained them in separate places; but often a dog broke loose at night and prowled around the caches. The other dogs then strained furiously at their chains, and half a dozen, breaking free, pounced on some detested enemy, rolled it over with their united weight, and ripped open its belly. Whoever first heard a chorus of howling outside immediately gave the alarm and, without waiting to dress, rushed into the midst of the fray, kicking and clubbing to right and left; yet even so we lost six dogs in the space of three months because we failed to turn out of our sleeping-bags in time. Idleness always breeds mischief; in summer the dogs fought for mere exercise, but in winter hard work quenched their lust for battle and made them content to sleep at night.

The time passed quickly, and almost before we realized it the land was buried in snow and the sea congealed into a solid field of ice. A stranded ice-hummock, more than a year old, supplied us with water, and the dogs grew familiar with their traces again from dragging the heavy blocks of ice to our tank. We expected each day to see the Eskimos of whom we had twice caught glimpses during the summer; but they failed to appear. At last I made ready a sled and dog-team to search for them forty miles to the westward around Stapylton Bay, Cox volunteering to accompany me, because it is never wise for a man to travel alone in the Arctic.

Our rations for the journey included a supply of white beans, which I determined to cook beforehand to save time and fuel on the trail. I carefully measured two gallons into a three-gallon pot, covered them with water, and set them to boil on the stove. But they seem to have swollen beyond my expectations, for my colleagues declared that before the afternoon ended I had filled every pot in the house, and commandeered every cauldron around the station in a vain effort to stem the rising tide.

We travelled three days, and found no Eskimos in the vicinity of Stapylton Bay. The ice was soft and sticky, but we struggled along to Hope Point, a distance of twenty-five miles. Before we reached the point a dark line in the sky above the horizon warned us that the sea was not everywhere covered with solid ice, and just beyond we came up against a great lead of water that stretched as far as the eye could see. Farther progress was useless and indeed impossible. The season was too early; no Eskimos would settle on the coast while the sea remained open. So we cached most of our pemmican on a low promontory and with lightened sled regained the station in one day.

Though we found no Eskimos on this short trip we learned two things that proved of value later. We discovered, first, that a single-walled tent is hardly comfortable in temperatures below the freezing-point. We had always used double tents in winter, but the mildness of the weather on this occasion tempted us to experiment with a Burberry tent, of single thickness, that weighed only thirteen pounds, and had a texture so close that it well-nigh excluded the light. A thick layer of frost settled over its inside the first night we set it up, and the slightest touch on the walls brought an icy shower upon our heads. The heat of the stove then changed the frost to water, which trickled over our sleeping-bags; and when the stove was out the inrush of cold air converted the water to ice, impossible to dislodge either by shaking or beating. So our thirteen-pound tent grew stiffer and heavier day by day, and weighed almost sixty pounds at the conclusion of the trip.

We learned further, what was perhaps of greater importance, that there were always enough sticks along this coast within a few hundred yards of any camping-spot to cook supper at night, dry all one's clothes, and then to cook breakfast in the morning. Unfortunately, with only a small oil-burning stove, we ourselves could make no use of it. We had left behind our usual travelling stove because wood had been scarce in the immediate vicinity of Bernard Harbour, and we feared that what little might lie on the beaches to the west would be buried beneath the snow. The primus stove cooked all our meals without much trouble, but would not dry our clothing; and to pull on frozen boots and mittens each morning was far from pleasant. Moreover, the coal-oil tainted the atmosphere of the tent and ruined my delicious beans. The next party travelling along this coast should discard the primus altogether and use a wood stove only.

The weather grew steadily colder after our return; in the space of a week the harbour ice increased in thickness from seven inches to two feet. We had long since given up all hope that Anderson's schooner, the *Alaska,* could return to Bernard Harbour before the next summer, and we wondered what had befallen her on the 1000-mile voyage. Chipman and O'Neill, who had orders to re-map the coast-line half-way to Herschel Island, decided to begin the work immediately and travel as far as Cape Lyon, or at least until they discovered some trace of our commander and his party.

They left us on November 18, just a week before the sun finally vanished for the winter. Cox and Johansen, who accompanied them for the first few miles, reported that their dogs were progressing steadily over smooth, hard snow at the rate of about three miles an hour. There now remained at the station only four men—Johansen, Cox, myself, and the Eskimo Palaiyak. The number was reduced to three a few days later, for the winter night was drawing near and my work called me away to the snow-huts of the Eskimos.

# CHAPTER III

## THE PEOPLE OF THE TWILIGHT

GLOOMY and barren seemed the country around Bernard Harbour when we first set foot upon its shore—a land of long twilights soon to be swallowed up in a longer night. A few vestiges of habitation there were—stone rings that marked old camping-sites, and shallow pits from which the hunters had launched their arrows at the passing caribou. But of the Eskimos themselves, of those dwellers in the twilight who even then were awaiting the dawn of the new age, we saw no sign.

It was they who discovered us a few days after our arrival, and sent two families down to reconnoitre. Their tent, nestling in a narrow fold among the ridges, caught the keen gaze of Anderson, who was gathering botanical specimens before sailing for the west. Two men armed with long knives advanced to meet him, and some women and children peered anxiously around the corner of the tent. He patted his chest and pronounced his name. Their expressions changed instantly, for Anderson had visited the Coppermine River three years before and his name had spread far and wide. "Andeseena," they cried. "It is Andeseena. We are glad, we are glad." Invited by gestures to accompany him down to the harbour, they followed with alacrity, and gathered on the beach beside our anchorage. We feasted them to their hearts' content, and gave them a few presents which, trifling enough to us, appeared in their eyes riches beyond measure. They left us the following day to return to the interior, and we saw them no more until the winter.

Another band heard of our friendliness and descended to the station in September. They halted when they saw Palaiyak and myself on the beach, and, standing in line on the ridge above, raised and lowered their hands to show that they held no weapons. We had been hunting seals, and carried rifles, which seemed to increase their nervousness; so we laid them on the ground and answered the peace-signal, repeating it two or three times as they anxiously awaited our approach. Dried fish and hard bread dissipated their fears, and some petty gifts unlocked both their tongues and their curiosity. They introduced their wives and children to us the next morning, and departed inland before noon to resume their caribou-hunting.

The timidity of these Eskimos came not from ordinary cowardice, but from a superstitious dread of the mysterious powers which they believed all white men possessed. The leader of the second band, whose right hand was tightly bandaged and whose thumb lay inside a small bag suspended from his neck, sufficiently attested their physical courage. Three weeks before he had stalked and wounded a grizzly, and when the infuriated animal attacked him he had thrown away his bow and killed it with his hunting-knife. His thumb was the price of the encounter, and he kept it as a souvenir. But a bear was a familiar adversary, a white man a being unknown; and this old hunter, who did not shrink from the grizzly, trembled with fear the first time I touched his arm.

Except for one other brief visit from the second band we saw no more of the Eskimos until the winter. Only Chipman, travelling far inland in search of caribou, encountered one of our early acquaintances packing dried fish from a cache. The Eskimo offered him a salmon rather heavily encrusted with mould, and Chipman returned the compliment by dividing up his sandwiches. Side by side they sat down on the edge of a lake to eat their lunch, though neither could understand a word of the other's language. *"Kovearnark-silekpakpogle,"* said the hunter to open up the conversation; and Chipman, not to be outdone, patted him on the back and responded, "Good for you, old fellow, good for you." Both broke into peals of laughter and repeated the performance. They separated at the conclusion of the feast, but the novel friendship persisted, and the hunter always treated "Hippimanna" as a brother whenever their paths happened to bring them together.

About the middle of November, when Chipman and O'Neill were outfitting for their journey, the Eskimos in the hinterland gave up caribou-hunting and settled on the coast to prepare for the sealing season. Five families who had built their snow-houses a few miles east of our station now paid us daily visits, and the women rendered good service by making us clothes and sleeping-bags from the raw furs we had brought on our schooners. They sewed most of these articles inside the station, where we provided the necessary needles and thread; and they behaved amazingly well, considering their inexperience of white men and the strangeness of the surroundings. Their broad, smiling faces enlivened our sober home, and their keen sense of humour led to many amusing incidents. They thought the panes of glass a novel kind of ice, and on their first visit could not distinguish the door from the rest of the house. "Knee," a comedian already admitted inside, laughed and gesticulated at them through the windows, and when they wandered round and round, seeking in vain for the entrance, gravely advised them to try the stove-pipe.

Their honesty, alas! was not above suspicion. Nor could we feel surprised. We were white men, beings of an unknown world, possibly their enemies. So many wonderful things lay in full view around them, things that we regarded but lightly or threw aside as worthless. One after another these began to disappear; first a few discarded tins, then some needles, then a spoon or two. We paid no heed for a time; but when more valuable articles vanished from the house we decided to watch our visitors. We knew they concealed the stolen goods on their persons, although we could discover no pockets in their fur clothing. Both sexes wore loose jackets like European swallow-tail coats, with hoods that pulled over the head. Their breeks, bound tightly round the hips, reached no lower than the knees; and their feet were encased in tight-fitting shoes of tanned sealskin. Yet there was one noticeable difference, for whereas the men had fur stockings tied above the calves, the women wore enormously wide "gum-boots" cut away on the inner sides so that a great pouch bulged out below each knee. We could find no reason for this feminine footgear until a woman slyly dropped a large cup into one pouch. Then we realized that it might have its uses, and solved the mystery of our stolen utensils.

It was these "gum-boots," perhaps, that made the women the worst offenders, sometimes the very women whom we least suspected. Palaiyak reported that he had seen one of our frying-pans in the hut of Mrs.

Light, a motherly old lady for whom we had entertained the greatest respect. It fell to my lot to recover
it, so I quietly asked her to bring back our *ookoosik,* as
the Eskimos call all cooking vessels. The old lady
smiled graciously and went home. Two hours later
she returned and handed me, not the frying-pan, but
an enormous four-gallon pot that, unknown to us,
she had also filched from one of our caches.

To distract their attention from our station and
caches I decided to study the natives at their own
homes, and to that end induced them to build me a
snow-hut. There I lived beside them for three days,
enjoying their hospitality and sharing their food as
they shared mine. Their life was very tranquil at this
period; the women stayed home and sewed, while the
men wandered back to a small lake and fished until
dark. In the evenings they questioned me about my
own country. Some of my food tasted good, they said,
especially the sugar; but why did I eat so much grass
(rice and oatmeal) instead of strong, nourishing meat?
Were seals and caribou not numerous in my land?
And my woollen clothes, from what strange skins did
they come? Were they the best garments that white
men could secure? Surely their own country was far
richer than mine.

They told me one evening of a large tribe that was
mustering on the opposite side of the strait, and a man
volunteered to guide me to the village. Together we

returned to the station, that I might prepare an outfit and leave with him early the next morning.

My guide was greatly alarmed when he found himself alone inside our house with three white men and an Eskimo from an unknown tribe. To calm his fears I showed him an old book about Greenland. A picture of a toy dog excited his curiosity, and he tried to take the animal up in his fingers. When the hour grew late we made him a bed on the floor beside Palaiyak; but he sat staring in front of him, too frightened to lie down. Palaiyak slept soundly; one after another the rest of us turned into our bunks and extinguished the lamps until only the night-light remained. The house was wrapped in silence; even the dogs outside lay still. At last he mustered up his courage, stretched himself out under the skins, and slumbered noisily.

We passed the first night in a snow-hut on one of the Liston and Sutton Islands, reaching the coast of Victoria Island late the next evening. There was no moon, but the dim light of the hurricane-lantern enabled my skilful companion to construct a new hut almost as quickly as by daylight. While he was building the walls I closed all the chinks and cracks with soft snow to keep out the cold air. I carefully adjusted, too, the snow-block that served as a door, for I was determined to be warmer this night than I had been the night before. We both slept soundly until morning, when I rose, lit the lantern, and tried to ignite the primus lamp. But the lamp refused to burn, and even the lantern began to go out. Then I realized that I had made the hut too air-tight, that the oxygen was exhausted, and that we would quickly smother unless we broke down the door and let in some fresh air.

Skirting the coast-line, we came upon fresh tracks leading away from a primitive fox-trap built of snow-blocks. Presently we sighted four men coming from different directions, who ran toward a common focus behind a ridge as soon as they noticed our sled. My companion raced ahead, flinging up his arms in the peace-signal as he, too, disappeared from my view. I followed more slowly with the dog-team, and, breasting the ridge, discovered the four strangers lined up as though on parade, the tallest man on the right. He announced his name, I told him mine, and, stepping down the line, introduced myself to the next man with as much formality as at a president's levee. But the last youth had three names, all very long; and he pronounced the three in one breath. My ears could not register so many ponderous syllables, and I said with a smile, "Phew, *takirut* (What long names)." The strangers gasped at this amazing breach of etiquette, but immediately saw the humour of the situation and laughed uproariously.

We approached their village in triumph, two of the men escorting me in front, two racing behind with my companion. Their twelve snow-huts lay at the bottom of the bay, where a band of children were rolling hoops along the ice of the foreshore. "White man, white man," my companions shouted as they ran. The villagers poured out of their houses and crowded around me, men jostling women, and women pushing aside men, in their eagerness to scan my face and tell me their names. At the last came a tall, dignified man of about middle age who warmly seized my arm and invited me to enter his hut. When I crawled in behind him he set me in the place of honour at the back of the sleeping-platform, dusted the snow from my shoes, and seated himself in front at my feet.

My guide had relatives in this village witn whom he proposed to spend the night; but I had many notes to write and desired a separate snow-hut where I could be quiet and undisturbed. The Eskimos gladly built one for me while I unharnessed and fed the dogs; and they vied with each other in unloading the sled, hoping to catch a glimpse of my trade goods. Some stayed to share my supper, boiled rice seasoned with sugar and canned milk; and it was amusing to watch their faces as each in turn swallowed a spoonful of the novel dish. Not all of them shared my own opinion of its excellence, and the discussion that arose about the white man's food might have lasted all night if the distant booming of a drum had not diverted their thoughts and brought about a hasty exodus. The people were holding a dance in my honour, and awaited my presence in the dance-house, which was in this village the forecourt of a large two-roomed hut. Seated in state on a sleeping-platform I watched their monotonous performance for two hours; then weariness overcame me, and, slipping through the low doorway, I retired, unattended, to my new home.

Eskimo dances have a superficial resemblance to the open-air meetings of a church army band, except that the only musical instrument is a drum. The singers form a ring around the leader, who hops and prances rhythmically to the accompaniment of a song. As one dancer tires and steps back into the ring, another takes his place. Women and children alternate with the men, for the sexes have almost equal status in this twilight land. Sometimes the faces of the singers glow with such earnestness that even the alien spectator succumbs to the emotional atmosphere and joins in their embryonic religion. Thus with song and dance they while away the evening hours until one after another drops out of the circle and the gathering dissolves to its homes

I measured the heads and statures of the Eskimos from carly the next morning until mid-afternoon. Every man who submitted to the operation received a fish-hook, every woman a needle; and the payment seemed to satisfy them all. On completing these measurements I traded for museum specimens, bartering knives, files, and other articles for lamps and pots of stone, ladles of musk-ox horn, and garments of seal-skin and caribou fur. The natives, growing more and more excited as my stock of trade goods diminished, jostled and clamoured for place, fearful of being too late for the bargains. Finally a riot threatened, and I resorted to strategy, stopping the trading to fill or relight my pipe whenever their emotions gained the upper hand. By evening I had exhausted all my goods and amassed enough specimens to fill my sled for the return journey.

Two of the villagers accompanied me back to the station, partly from curiosity, partly to gain the advantages of early trading. They were not the representatives I myself would have chosen, for they were young and inexperienced, with all the presumption that often goes with youth. The size of our outfit awed them a little the first day, and the many strange instruments set up around the station amazed and bewildered them. But their embarrassment passed away overnight; consumed by curiosity, they wanted to handle everything they saw and begged continually for whatever seized their fancy. Palaiyak was quite disgusted with them. He told them about the missionaries who were coming the following year, men who would teach them the good life that led after death to the sky. But our guests assured him they had no desire to go to sky-land; they were content with their own country, which contained enough seals and caribou to satisfy all their needs.

I intended to revisit the settlement on Victoria Island at the earliest opportunity, but preferred to choose my own travelling companions. Our guests therefore returned alone, while I arranged to spend a few days in the hut of the leader of our local tribe. My host, the hero of the skirmish with the grizzly, had now recovered the use of his right hand, and was preparing to cross to the Liston and Sutton Islands for the seal-hunt, since it was still too early in the winter to build a hut on the sea-ice far away from land. He suggested that I should join his train to the islands and push on later to Victoria Island, which was but thirty-five miles beyond; and as the invitation accorded well with my plans I accepted gladly.

The wife of my host was Light, the lady who had filched the pot and the frying-pan from our station. It has not been my habit to lodge among thieves, but my experience on this occasion was most encouraging. Light was charming as a hostess. She licked my plate before each meal that I might eat from a clean dish, and when handing me boiled seal meat from her steaming pot she squeezed it tenderly between thumb and forefinger that no surplus juice might drip on my clothing. Lacking candy, she showered on me the national substitute, delicate cubes of oily seal-blubber;

but, lacking the national taste, I slipped most of them surreptitiously to the dogs.

Two of the five families in this tribe crossed to the islands a day earlier than the others. I accompanied the second party, which started out in the darkness of the morning. After traversing the first nine miles without difficulty we came upon rough ice that had been piled into jagged hummocks by the autumn gales, and my light sled, modelled after a European pattern, upset three times before we passed through. The Eskimo sleds were more stable, for their crossbars rested directly on the stout runners, and with the heavier articles, such as stone lamps and bales of meat and blubber, lying at the bottom, the centre of gravity was close to the ground. None of them overbalanced, although they were piled six feet high with the household possessions.

The nearest of the islands was Putulik, "the island pierced with a hole"; for legend stated that a large cave extended under the water from one side to the other. We approached it shortly before dark, and my host sent forward his twelve-year-old son to pick out a house-site. The inexperienced lad chose a spot where the snow was too shallow, but his father, sounding the depth all around with a long stick of antler, quickly found a more suitable location. While the men erected their huts, the women built low ramparts around the outer walls to increase the warmth inside and to serve as storage-places for the bales of clothing. In little more than an hour the lamps burned brightly again in every home and we were dining sumptuously on dried trout and frozen salmon.

The snow-hut of the Eskimo is too well known to require a detailed description. It resembles the upper half of a sphere, slightly flattened at the top, with a diameter at the floor level of about nine feet and a maximum height slightly below six. A low platform covered with musk-ox and caribou robes takes up more than half the floor space; it serves as a bed by night and a place for sitting and working during the day. The entrance, which faces the middle of the platform, is simply a hole at the bottom of the wall large enough for a person to crawl through on hands and knees; a single snow-block at night makes a satisfactory door. To the right (or left) of the entrance is the saucer-shaped lamp for burning seal-blubber; the stone cooking-pot hangs over it, and over the pot is a large tray or rack where boots and mittens are spread out to dry. A table between the lamp and the sleeping-platform completes the furniture, but bags containing meat and blubber, and dishes of various kinds, litter the floor on both sides of the entrance. Finally, a low-roofed passage extending outward from the doorway ten to thirty feet leads into the open air.

The adjoining plan of a two-roomed hut, and the photographs scattered throughout the book, will give a better idea of its shape and internal arrangements than a lengthy description. Theoretically a snow-hut may be of any size, provided you have ladders, or timber to form a staging. The Eskimos have neither. To build a large dance-hall like that shown in the plan they stand on boxes, bales of clothing, and anything that may be available. So the height of their largest hut never exceeds eight feet, and the diameter is limited to correspond. Being a sociable people, however, two families often share a single dwelling, and two or three others arrange their huts so that they open onto the same passage.

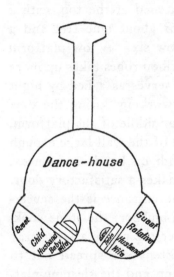

Dance-house

Imagine us, then, sitting on the edge of the sleeping-platform eating our supper, myself at one end of the line, Mrs. Light at the other facing her table and lamp. The different members of the family are grouped between us, two boys, a grown-up nephew, and lastly Mrs. Light's husband, who naturally has a seat beside his wife. The youngest boy carries presents of fish to the inmates of the other huts, and two little girls who return with him, bringing similar offer-

ings for us, stand shyly inside the doorway, kicking
their feet together restlessly as though knocking off
the snow. Every one is tired after the day's journey,
and as soon as the meal is ended strips off his clothes,
tucks them under his head for a pillow, and glides into
a sleeping-bag of caribou fur. Mrs. Light is the last
to retire, for she still has some small duties to perform.
She calls in the dogs from the passageway, one by
one, throws them a few strips of blubber, and drives
them out with the snow-duster, a short stick for beating the snow from our garments. Then she adjusts
the lamp for the night, turns our boots and mittens so
that they will dry on both sides, fits the snow-block
into the doorway to keep out the cold air and the dogs,
and slips quickly into her husband's "double" bag of
caribou fur. Most of the inmates sleep with their
mouths open, and their loud snores reverberating
inside the hut drown the less resonant notes of the
dogs in the passage.

Leaving Putulik, I rejoined my late acquaintances
on Victoria Island. The sun no longer climbed above
the horizon, and the "day" was limited to the twilight
hours from 9:30 A.M. to 2:30 P.M.; but a bright moon
lit up the trail for me during the last three hours of
the journey. The tribe was still living in the same
settlement, for the women had not completed all the
new fur clothes their families required during the winter months, and it would violate one of their most

rigid taboos to finish the sewing on the sea-ice. My old snow-hut was empty as I had left it, but cold and cheerless without the warm glow of a blubber-lamp. Seeking more comfort in an inhabited hut, I became the "guest" of a man named Snow-Knife, sharing my food with his family and giving them presents from time to time in payment for occupying half their dwelling. The arrangement proved fairly satisfactory for two or three weeks, but later in the winter I changed my quarters and lodged with another family more sensitive to my personal comfort than to my worldly possessions.

The women sewed industriously from morning till night, but the men found the time drag heavily. Some of them were still bringing in the caribou meat they had cached during the summer, and the pokes of blubber left on the coast in the spring. A few set fox-traps obtained the previous winter from Captain Bernard, the first and only trader who had visited their country. The rest stayed quietly at home and put their sealing-gear in order, or helped their wives to scrape the caribou hides.

In one hut that I visited a middle-aged Eskimo was trying to repair a 30.30 Winchester rifle he had purchased from Captain Bernard. A bullet had stuck in the barrel, for, like many a more civilized hunter, he had scrupulously oiled the outside of the weapon, but entirely neglected the inside. He hammered on the bullet with his ramrod; when that failed, he borrowed another rifle and fired a blank cartridge down the muzzle, while a crowd of natives stood around him to see the result. Fortunately there were no casualties; the chamber merely swelled to the size of a hen's egg and cracked. Then the man and his companions, thinking that the tempered steel might be malleable like the native copper they used for their tools, attempted to weld the crack by pounding on it with a heavy stone.

Hitherto I had escaped all friction with the natives; now came my first trouble. I was sitting in their largest hut, bartering knives, files, and cooking-pots for the usual museum specimens. A native offered to exchange a small horn drinking ladle for a twelve-inch butcher's knife, and I refused, since the knife was worth a dozen such ladles. He knew that all my companions were fifty miles away, and determined to take by force what he was unable to obtain through barter. He seized the knife, and I seized his wrist. In strength we were equally matched; he could not release his wrist, nor could I force the knife out of his fingers. The hut was crowded to suffocation with Eskimos, who made no attempt to take part in the struggle, but waited to see the issue. They had no chief, no one with authority to settle the case at strife; if my adversary won, the more lawless would band together and strip me of everything I had. The situation seemed desperate as I played my last card. Looking sternly into the man's eyes, I intoned in English, slowly and deliberately, "If—you—do—not —hand—over—that—knife—there—will—be—no— more—trade—between—your — people—and—my— people."

The effect of these words was magical. The natives, understanding no English, thought them a curse that would bring some dire calamity upon their heads. My adversary was terrified. He glanced at his kinsmen uneasily, not knowing what might happen to him the next minute; but—he still clung to the knife. Then the owner of the hut caught hold of his arm and ordered him to release the weapon. It dropped from his fingers, and he pushed through the crowd to the doorway. Not until many weeks later did he venture to appear in my presence again, or to visit our station at Bernard Harbour.

I refused to trade for some days after this incident, and threatened to cut off all trade at Bernard Harbour during the winter. The loss to the Eskimos would have been infinitely greater than to us, because there were only three things we wished to purchase— caribou meat for ourselves, seal meat for the dogs, and museum specimens. The natives, on the contrary, had many wants; they cried insistently for steel knives, iron pots, and metal goods of every description, but above all for rifles and ammunition to replace their bows and arrows. We had supplies in abundance to cover most of their needs; but the other members of our party spoke no Eskimo, and had gladly delegated all the trading to me after the first day's experience. Anderson, who joined us at Christmas, approved the arrangement, which held throughout the duration of the expedition. It placed a power in my hands that increased my security among the natives and rescued me from more than one awkward predicament. On this occasion the mere cessation of trade for a few days quelled their aggressiveness and checked any further attempt at open robbery.

As soon as the majority of the women had finished their sewing, the Eskimos began to migrate along the coast to a low promontory from which they could cross in one day to the Liston and Sutton Islands. They moved on different mornings, and at different hours of the morning, some early and some late. Their only clocks were the sun by day and the moon and stars by night; but the sun had now disappeared for several weeks, the moon set early, and the stars do not shine through walls of snow. So my host, who wished to set out at daybreak, roused his household nearly three hours too soon; and his grievous error made us shiver in idleness on the sleeping-platform until it grew light enough to load up the sleds.

The villagers were too practical to carry all the furniture out through the long passageways when they abandoned their huts. Those who had windows of ice in their houses removed them and passed their goods through the gap; and those who had no windows cut large holes in the walls, which they could fill up with a snow-block or two if they wanted to reoccupy the huts. But the Eskimos seldom returned to the same habitations; old houses remained deserted until the spring, when they melted slowly away under the warm rays of the sun. Passing travellers might occupy them for a night, but even they generally preferred to build new houses, which were warmer and more comfortable. Hence one could readily discover all the winter movements of these Eskimos by tracking down the villages they had successively deserted between October and May.

Our migration along the coast resulted in a new settlement of snow-huts a few yards out from the beach. It was too early in the winter to camp far from shore, for a violent gale might break the level ice-field into drifting floes. Even the light gale that sprang up four nights later produced a large tide-crack under two houses that lay more to seaward than the rest. Misfortune ruled that I should be sleeping in one of them. The snow-blocks cracked one after another, with loud reports like pistol-shots, and the walls split from ceiling to floor. Then the water poured up through the tide-crack and flooded the hut nearly to the level of the sleeping-platform. My hostess, stepping down to relight the lamp, sank up to her knees in the icy slush; her terrified shriek made us leap from our beds in alarm. Fortunately the water rose no higher during the night, or we might have had difficulty in escaping to the land. As it was we were able to wait until daylight, when we cut a hole through the back wall and transported our belongings to a safer home beyond the reach of the tide.

I marvelled at the time that the roof of the dwelling did not cave in upon our heads. But a snow-hut is remarkably solid once the warmth inside has converted its walls to ice. Soon after this gale I visited the hut in which I was nearly asphyxiated a few weeks before, and the native who accompanied me stood on its highest block without disaster. He mounted cautiously, it is true, for even ice must be fairly thick to withstand a pressure of 150 pounds; and the walls of this hut were still mainly snow, for we had occupied it only one night. But it was a striking test of the solidity of a snow-house, and explained why the entire half of a dwelling may be cut away without disturbing the other half.

There were so many things of interest in our new settlement, so much that was novel and strange to record in my note-books each evening, that the days passed almost unnoticed. The Eskimos themselves knew nothing of days or weeks; they kept no reckoning even of the months, only of the changing seasons as they affected the food supply. But my diary warned me that the time was speeding, and that I must hitch up my dog-team if I intended to join my comrades in their Christmas dinner.

December 20 saw my sled heading across the ice toward Putulik. One can usually cross from this island to Bernard Harbour in five hours; but the recent gale had piled up a pressure ridge a hundred yards wide, and I laboured with my axe for three hours before I could work through its hummocks. It was late in the evening when I reached our station. My team, excited by the light in the window, raced madly toward the shore, the dogs tethered on the beach barked furiously, and Cox and Johansen stumbled out of the house to welcome me home again. Like a prodigal son returning from a far-distant country, I was pushed indoors to rest after the journey while they unloaded my sled and attended to the needs of the dogs.

Photo by F. Johansen.

Running down to the barrier of floes, we tried to force our way through.

Photo by F. Johansen.

The wall sagged in the middle of one side through the weight of an enormously thick rampart of turf.

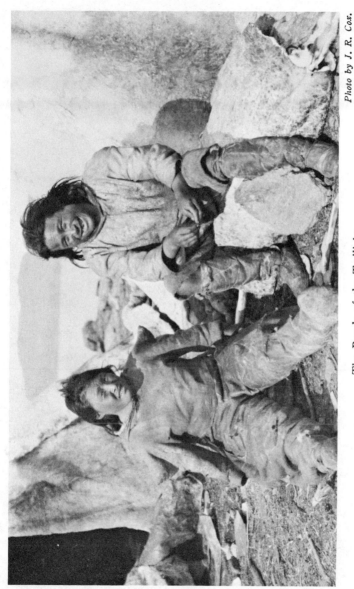

Photo by J. R. Cox.

The People of the Twilight.

The snow-hut.

They built their settlement close to the beach.

We distributed our loads in the proportion of a hundred pounds for each dog.

Wives and daughters pulled in front of the dogs.

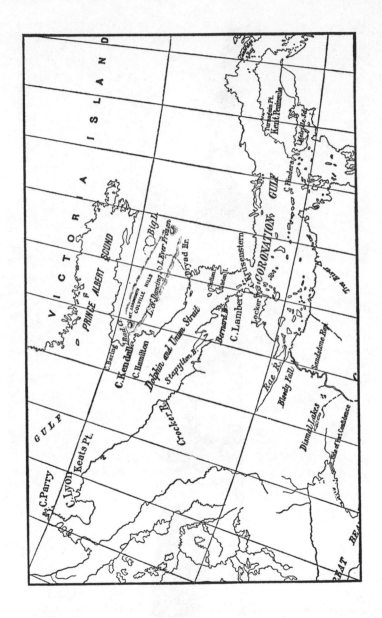

## CHAPTER IV

## AMONG THE SNOW-HUTS

OUTWARDLY the station had undergone a great change during my absence. The snow was everywhere, the land and sea merged into one another. Only the pillars for the thermometers and anemometer, and the section of stove-pipe above the roof, stood out like sentries on the crest of the low ridge, guarding the dark lines of the dogs. The caches lay swallowed up in the general whiteness except where a straight-edged box rested on the extreme top of a pile; and the turf that covered the walls and roof of the house was concealed by the all-pervading snow, which daily mounted nearer the window-sills.

We rose early on Christmas morning, although we

felt anything but merry with half our party somewhere
in the unknown. About 8 :30 A.M. came the first glim-
merings of dawn. The sun would not rise all day, but
we should have five hours of twilight sufficient for
working outdoors, though not for reading inside the
house. Cox wandered away to visit his fox-traps,
Johansen prepared the dinner, and I set about mending my sled. Suddenly Cox reappeared at the western
entrance of the harbour, racing in front of two sleds;
behind him trudged Anderson, Chipman, and O'Neill,
with three other men, Castel the seaman, Sullivan (or
"Cockney") the cook of the *Alaska,* and a western
Eskimo named Ikey. Chipman and O'Neill going
west had encountered Anderson coming east at Keats'
Point. They had turned back with him, and by forced
marches the two parties had now reached home again
just in time to share our Christmas celebration.

We did celebrate, too, although our bill of fare was
in no way lengthy. Anderson circulated a small bottle
of wine, the second of three furnished to us for
"medicinal" purposes; and we dined triumphantly on
a hind-quarter of venison, dehydro potatoes, canned
peas, and rice pudding. He had found no mail at
Herschel Island, but we hardly felt the disappointment, so relieved were we to have him back again and
to know that the *Alaska* was safe in its winter quarters
at Baillie Island. We wound up the day with a Christmas cake presented to us eighteen months before by

some friends in British Columbia, and felt our isolation slip away for a few hours as we joined with the rest of the Christian world in common festival.

Our enlarged party now required more accommodation, so the store became a kitchen fitted with bunks for Castel and Cockney. The two western Eskimos, Palaiyak and Ikey, slept in a tent surrounded by snow-walls covered with a tarpaulin roof. The house itself was reserved for the six members of the scientific staff. That, at least, was our intention; but unfortunately the natives around us were too civilized to read the notice on the door, and inundated our hut as frequently as before.

Christmas ended, I returned to my Eskimos at Putulik, in the Liston and Sutton Islands, taking Palaiyak as assistant and interpreter. The natives whom I had visited on Victoria Island had also gathered there, so that the settlement now consisted of some thirty families living in twenty-five snow-huts. We erected our tent right in their midst, and built a snow-hut over it, both for warmth and for extra storage-room between the two walls. Not wishing to violate any of their customs concerning the sharing of food, we entertained two or three visitors at every meal, and distributed the scraps among the crowd at the door. Trading and visiting among the houses occupied most of the day-time; but after the hunters returned from their sealing we attended the celebrations in the dance-house, or gathered the elder men inside our tent and enquired into their customs and beliefs.

Compared with the Eskimos of Alaska, these natives were astonishingly primitive. Their language contained no word for any number beyond six. I induced a woman to count on her fingers, and she began, in her own tongue, "one, two, one." I corrected her, and she started again, "one, two, three." There she stopped, and a man standing beside her said "four." Both had forgotten the words for the next two numbers, considering everything above four as many. Yet they were not so primitive as to be easily short-changed in any transaction, for they could separate a pile of articles into groups of three or four and count them with tolerable accuracy. A man to whom I gave only nineteen cartridges instead of twenty fitted them into an empty box, discovered the error, and indignantly demanded the missing round.

These people lacked, too, the artistic skill for which their kinsmen in other places are famous. I distributed pencils and paper to several adults, both men and women, and asked them to draw sketches of people, houses, caribou, and anything else they cared to attempt. The results were amusing, similar to what we should expect from a child of six. Even my chart they were unable to follow. One man, more intelligent than the rest, seemed to grasp that a certain line might represent the coast along which he had recently been travelling; but when I asked him to name and point out the positions of the capes and streams he had passed on the way, he placed his finger indifferently on places as far apart as Victoria Island and Great Bear Lake. Yet an Eskimo of northern Alaska, who was unable to read and had never held a pencil in his hand, once drew me a remarkably accurate outline of the Colville River and all its tributaries, besides many vivid sketches of camp scenes and the hunting of seals and caribou.

Among the specimens I bought at this time was a large lamp which we immediately put to use for warming up our tent. It was made from soft soapstone, and shaped like an enormous saucer cut in half. We filled it with crushed seal-blubber, and along the straight front edge arranged the wick of cotton-grass seeds, which are not unlike cotton-wool. The lamp, when burning perfectly, gave a low smokeless flame an inch high and about sixteen inches long, quite sufficient to keep us comfortably warm even with the door partly open; but as neither Palaiyak nor I were very skilful in adjusting the wick a thin layer of soot began to form over the inside of the tent. We hired two little girls to keep the dogs away when we were absent, and my "daughters," as the people laughingly called them, gradually assumed responsibility also for the lamp, which they managed to perfection. I rewarded them on the first occasion by holding a private party at which they shared the white man's food—tea, hard bread, and chocolate. When I left them in charge again the following day they immediately trimmed the lamp, placed a pot of water over the flame to boil, and set out the cups for another afternoon tea.

These Eskimos of Dolphin and Union Strait forbade any cooking of caribou meat on the sea during the winter months, believing that it would cause the ice under their settlement to upheave and engulf them. Eskimos living farther to the eastward were less scrupulous, and often cooked caribou meat when they were camped on bay ice that was not likely to crack under the stress of a winter storm. But a strong current passes through Dolphin and Union Strait, and new cracks and pressure ridges make their appearance as late as the end of January. The regulation was therefore rigidly observed by the local Eskimos, who often warned us against infringing it at Putulik, even though their settlement was only a few yards from the shore. Palaiyak, my western Eskimo, who had outgrown most of these superstitions, was more annoyed than I that we should be compelled to eat our venison raw, or else carry it to Bernard Harbour, where our house was built on solid ground. We avoided the regulation in the following winter by a subterfuge. The Eskimos then built their settlement closer to the beach, and the hut in which we were living had rock, not ice, beneath the snow-floor, making the prohibition technically invalid. We cooked our caribou meat with easy consciences, and, when the natives upbraided us, pointed to a tiny patch of gravel exposed beneath our feet. Some accepted our verdict, most of them still disapproved; but by that time they were better acquainted with the strange ways of the white man, and believed that we could do with impunity what they could not attempt without disaster.

The village dance-house formed as usual the forecourt of two snow-huts, which kept it at an even temperature with their two large blubber-lamps. One hut was occupied by Ikpuckhuak, the elderly man who had come to my rescue when his fellow-tribesman tried to carry off my knife. Ikpuckhuak means the "Dirty One"; but the name in no wise reflected on his personal characteristics, for the Eskimos were too familiar with the lack of water during seven months of the year to pay much attention to some of its consequences. Ikpuck, as I shall call him hereafter, was actually cleaner than most of his countrymen, provided one gives the word a rather broad interpretation; and his name was no more than an ancient family title which he inherited in childhood along with his other privileges.

We spent several pleasant evenings on his sleeping-platform, reclining comfortably on caribou robes and listening to the natives in the forecourt singing their monotonous songs to the accompaniment of a drum. At times their dances were interspersed with strange religious ceremonies, always fascinating to watch and occasionally difficult to comprehend. They knew nothing of Christianity. Their forefathers had taught them to believe in a goddess dwelling at the bottom of the sea who controlled both the winter storms and the supply of seals. They did not worship her as we understand worship, but they held her in great awe, and often tried to secure her goodwill by persuasion or by threats. Many of their misfortunes were laid directly to her door; others were ascribed to the spirits of the dead, or to the machinations of sorcerers. Their sole defence against these imaginary foes lay in their shamans or medicine-men, who claimed to summon into their bodies powerful spirits of men and animals that had voluntarily placed themselves under human control. The medicine-men were thus the physicians, the prophets, and the priests of their little communities. Speaking as the mouthpieces of their spirits, they elucidated the past and foretold the future; and they sent their protecting spirits to bring back the stolen souls of the sick or to compel the sea-goddess to deliver up the seals she withheld from the starving Eskimos. Yet there were many occasions in life when even they could give no assistance, and the people, realizing this, accepted their fate with the fortitude customary to their race.

At the first dance we attended, a medicine-man gave an exhibition of his powers on behalf of two natives who had failed to capture any seals. He made a short speech from the centre of the ring, but suddenly broke off with a cry of pain and covered his eyes with his hands. Low groans shook his body; the protecting spirit that entered him seemed to rack his frame with agony. He raised his head and stared at us, his eyes wild with frenzy and his mouth working convulsively, although not a sound escaped his lips. The spectators on every side flung questions at him, and he turned eagerly from one to another, nodding his head whenever the answer was "Yes." In this way he informed us that two men had died recently somewhere to the eastward. The first spirit then left him as suddenly as it had entered, and a second, that took its place, restored his power of speech, but left his frenzy unchanged. In a weak falsetto he announced that the two hunters had alarmed the seals with a hatchet, but that the protecting spirit speaking through his lips had now removed the curse, and their next seal-hunt would be successful.

The medicine-man's performance lasted over half an hour, two or three more spirits taking possession of him in quick succession. The last refused to depart, and made him stagger so heavily that I thought he would faint. The spectators asked me to tap him on the head with some matches, those marvellous fire-sticks that only the white man knew how to manufacture; but even they were not powerful enough to restore his wandering senses. Perhaps my hand would be more efficacious. I laid it on his temple, and saw his eyes rest on me without a gleam of intelligence. Then the madness passed out of them, a pleased smile broke over his countenance, and, quietly turning away, he began a casual conversation with some of the bystanders.

Performances of this kind revealed to me the heart of Eskimo religion. The natives trusted in their medicine-men, and the medicine-men, with rare exceptions, believed themselves gifted with supernatural powers. The spirits that wander unseen came at their bidding and obeyed their commands. At times they came unsummoned, and a man raved on the hill-sides or on the frozen sea where no one beheld his frenzy. Hysteria is peculiarly common around the Polar basin; the long winter darkness and the loneliness and silence of the hunter's life make the Arctic peoples more susceptible to this disorder than the rest of the human race. So religion and hysteria went closely hand in hand.

After measuring all the adults in this village I arranged with a native to guide me to another some forty miles farther west. We had travelled about half a mile when, looking back, I noticed with surprise that a woman was following in our trail. I turned to my guide and asked, "Who is this woman, and why does she follow us?" "It's only Snow-Knife's wife," he answered. "She is coming with us to visit her two sisters. Don't trouble about her. She will stay with me throughout our journey, and in the meantime my wife will live with Snow-Knife."

Marriage here was evidently not the institution we are taught to reverence. This woman had openly traded husbands for a few days in order to visit her relatives; and there were times when men seemed to exchange wives without even that excuse. I had read of the custom in books, but its impression was different when it occurred before my own eyes without the least attempt at concealment. It became more intelligible later, with fuller knowledge of their domestic life. The people were not really immoral, for they were doing no wrong according to the standards of life handed down to them through countless generations; and the transfer of wedlock was not made indiscriminately, but according to definite regulations. A man often had wives in half a dozen different tribes, some of whom he saw only once in his lifetime; and the wives had other husbands. But their children were all his children, forbidden to marry one another; and if ever he visited the tribe to which one of his wives belonged he received a cordial welcome, and was free to hunt and seal in its territory like the regular members of the community. A stranger in an Eskimo tribe was a potential enemy who could be killed at sight; but by this system of temporarily exchanging wives the natives could travel in safety from one end of the country to the other.

So Mrs. Snow-Knife, or Mrs. Wealthy, as she now became for a few days, accompanied us to the village of the "People of the Land on the Other Side." She arranged the skins and meagre furniture of our snow-huts, tended the lamp, and boiled the seal meat for our evening meal. I witnessed her meeting with her two sisters, one much older than herself, the other a maiden of about fifteen years. She herself rejoiced without effusion; the maiden displayed more interest in the white man's sled than in the sister of whom she had heard nothing for nine months; but the eldest woman sat in her hut and wept copiously throughout the evening. They were typically human in their outlooks, these three sisters dwelling where the midday twilight and the midnight sun follow each other season after season. The young girl was just beginning life and her hopes were all in the future; Mrs. Snow-Knife had been married several years and held both the past and the future in an equal balance; but the eldest woman, though still in the prime of life, bore the stamp of hardship on her face and her mind was already looking backward.

The "People of the Land on the Other Side" were too hospitable not to hold the usual dance in our honour. They had built no dance-house, and did not possess a drum; but about thirty squeezed into an ordinary dwelling-house eleven feet in diameter, where they banged my frying-pan and sang at the tops of their voices until the snow-ceiling, melting with the warmth of so many human beings, began to drip ice-cold water on our heads. The din and odour were terrific, more than flesh and blood could endure; so, pushing my way through the crowd, I retired to the purity of the outer air and gradually regained my senses.

We remained in this village one day and two nights while I measured all its adult inhabitants. Seal meat was not plentiful, and a longer stay would have left my dogs without food. Moreover, it was not necessary, for I was now formally introduced to the people, and could study them at my leisure when they joined the other two tribes in the Liston and Sutton Islands at the end of the month.

My party on the return journey was increased by three—Wealthy's cousin, whose wife was already at the island village, and two girls, Mrs. Snow-Knife's sister and another, who were bound on the high-road to matrimony. The brides piled everything they owned on top of my sled, which creaked and groaned under the extra load. Luckily their trousseaux were not as formidable as their white sisters', or we should never have reached our journey's end. The average Eskimo bride requires only four things—a meat-knife, a sewing-kit, a lamp, and a cooking-pot. Everything else—the home, skins, tools, and weapons—the bridegroom supplies, and in exceptional cases even the cooking-pot and the lamp.

We travelled as long as there was twilight, passing the snow-hut we had made on the outward journey and building a new one a few miles beyond. There was much confusion when the six of us gathered inside to eat our supper; but the confusion grew worse when we tried to settle down for the night, because the hut, erected in the darkness, was too small, and we could not all stretch out on the platform with our heads toward the door. Finally we compromised. Wealthy's cousin, who had no sleeping-gear, sat up all night, while I turned my bag the other way and slept with my head unpleasantly close to the back wall. Even so we were squeezed as tightly as books on a shelf. There were certainly no regrets when morning came and we set the sled in motion again.

The girls married a few weeks later. To the best of my knowledge one remained quite satisfied with the husband of her choice, or rather with the husband her relatives selected, for maidens seldom had the liberty to choose for themselves. The other fared differently. Her husband, after living with her for nine months, sent her away on that familiar plea, "incompatibility of temperament." Her adopted father then married her to his nephew, who divorced her within three weeks for the same reason. Since she was barely fifteen years of age even after her second marriage, and could easily secure a third husband whenever she wished, we persuaded her relatives to grant her a year of freedom. Childhood came back to her during these months of respite; and no girl in the country seemed happier. Finally she married a young Eskimo brought in by some traders from the Mackenzie River delta; but of her subsequent history I have no record.

Palaiyak and I returned to Bernard Harbour about the middle of January, for Anderson wished me to join him on a trip up the Coppermine River. We conducted to our station an Eskimo family and Ikpuck's step-daughter Sculpin, one of the two little girls who had tended my blubber-lamp. Scuplin, or Jennie, as my colleagues christened her, became a general favourite through her frank smile and merry laughter. More intelligent than most of her people, she knew how to keep out of our way, and spent many quiet hours in a corner mending the rents in our clothing, or gazing at the pictures in our books.

My scientific equipment included an Edison recording phonograph and a number of blank cylinders. Now that I had gathered at the station a small party of Eskimos easily handled and fairly familiar with our ways I used the opportunity to record some of their dance-songs. The Eskimos had paid little attention to the gramophone of Captain Bernard, our predecessor in this region, because they failed to understand the white man's music; but they looked with awe on the uncanny machine that reproduced not only their words but even the ejaculations that unconsciously escaped their lips. The first man who sang into it shivered with apprehension when he heard his voice come back to him out of the horn, and asked in an anxious whisper, "Is there a spirit concealed in the box?" Nothing would induce him to sing again, and for a time I feared that this first record of their music would also be my last. But little Jennie rose to the occasion; she was too young and innocent to fear the white men who had hitherto done them no harm, and the phonograph was an exciting adventure. She sang half a dozen chants for me that evening, and made the house ring with laughter when we played them over again, and she heard the coughing that interspersed the words. Thenceforward I had no difficulty in finding singers, and we carried out of the country records of 150 songs for future study.

Palaiyak and I paid another brief visit to the island Eskimos before travelling eastward. Jennie went back with us, and we lodged in the house of Ikpuck, her step-father, because it was more convenient than a private hut that needed constant guarding. Ikpuck's wife was a comely matron, weighing something under 200 pounds, who rejoiced in the possession of two

names, Liver and Icehouse. Both seemed rather mis-
leading; she was really neither choleric nor frigid, but
a jolly, high-spirited old lady with the warmest heart
imaginable, and a tongue more prone to gossip than was
strictly advisable. She received us with open arms,
and resigned to us half the platform in her hut, where
we slept and stored all our possessions. Since her
platform looked directly into the dance-house, the
centre of social life, we saw everything that happened
in the community, or heard it reported to our neighbours.

January was generally the coldest, darkest, and
stormiest month in the year, the only month that the
Eskimos really dreaded. Blizzards often confined
them to their houses five days out of seven, and even
if a hunter braved the storms he could find no seal-
holes through the driving snow. Hunger then reigned
in every hut, and the inmates shivered with cold as they
extinguished their lamps one by one to conserve the
oil. But the winter of 1914-15 was unusually mild.
Blizzards were rare even in January, and they were
separated by periods of calm weather when the hunters
captured five and six seals daily. So the lamps burned
brightly in all the houses and the natives were light-
hearted and happy. They gaily assembled in the dance-
house each evening to while away the hours with song
and dance; and their medicine-men often gave weird
performances, not to relieve distress, but simply to
maintain their prestige and entertain their audiences.

A little sickness was inevitable in the circumstances of their lives, and the medicine-men conjured in vain over one man who was slowly dying of a malady I myself could not diagnose. Several natives had coughs and colds, the result of changing from the outdoor life of summer to the seclusion of the winter hut. Ikpuck himself suffered from rheumatism, and borrowed my belt for a season that the vitality in my body might be transmitted to his own. Another invalid, the medicine-men said, was cured by Jumbo, my dog, who retrieved and restored his wandering soul. In gratitude they tied a band of soft white fur around the dog's neck to keep out the cold. Yet none of their ailments appeared serious except that of the dying man; and his had lasted too long to cloud the cheerfulness that pervaded the little community.

I revealed to the villagers my intention of travelling eastward, to visit some of their countrymen. They tried hard to dissuade me, asserting that the natives around the Coppermine River were so unfriendly toward white men that it would hardly be safe to venture among them. Of course, what concerned them was not my personal safety so much as the loss of trade through my absence, and the competition from the large body of eastern natives who would immediately flock to Bernard Harbour. They altered their tactics when they found that dissuasion was useless, and even heaped on me a number of petty commissions. One woman gave me a knife to present to a kinsman, another a pair of sealskin slippers; and so many sent messages that I kept a special memorandum of them all in my note-book.

One commission, and one alone, I declined to take upon my shoulders, although petitioned by an old, old man whose voice quavered so that it was hard to refuse him. He besought me to restore his widowed daughter, who lived somewhere to the eastward; to load her property upon my sled, share my tent with her, and bring her safely to his home. The task was beyond my capacity, but I referred it to our party at the station, and proposed that one of my colleagues should rescue the distressed lady. The choice fell on Johansen, whose beard was long and fatherly. But Johansen demurred, claiming that a younger knight, Cox or O'Neill, was more fitted for such an enterprise. They, too, drew back; one and all ungallantly refused their aid. When I met the woman later in Coronation Gulf, she proved to be the greasiest and worst-favoured native along the entire Arctic coast!

The Eskimos had no word for farewell in their language, but came and went without ceremony. We left them in the same way, hitching up our dog-team early in the morning and crossing the narrow strait to our station.

# CHAPTER V

## UP THE COPPERMINE RIVER

**A**N Arctic winter brings nothing but dreariness and ennui to an ardent zoologist. The birds have migrated to warmer climes, except a few ptarmigan, an occasional raven, and the solitary snowy owl. Bears, squirrels, lemmings, and mice have denned themselves up in their holes; most of the caribou have retreated to the Barren Lands far to the south; and only the fox, the hare, and the wolf contend with man against the winter storms. One may travel a hundred miles without finding a single track to break the monotonous surface of the snow.

Anderson, always energetic, had chafed under this forced inactivity ever since his arrival at Christmas. He could do very little zoological work around Bernard Harbour or Coronation Gulf until the spring; so why should he not take a mail out to Fort Norman?— five hundred miles away at the western extremity of Great Bear Lake. Our orders stated that mail should be forwarded to the government on every possible occasion, but hitherto we had not been able to report our safe arrival at Bernard Harbour and the progress of our scientific work. The first three months of the year, it is true, are not the most favourable for travelling; the days are short, the weather stormy, and the snow, away from the coast, both soft and deep. But even if he were unable to reach Fort Norman, the constant travelling would harden the dogs for their strenuous work in the long, mild days of spring; and the problem of feeding them would really be simplified, since caribou abounded in the valley of the Coppermine River throughout the winter, whereas at Bernard Harbour we had to purchase seal meat from the Eskimos. All things considered, it seemed advisable to undertake the journey. The seaman, Castel, was an efficient companion who could easily be spared from the station; myself and the Eskimo Palaiyak could form a supporting party to freight some of the supplies part of the distance and to establish caches of food against their return; and Johansen could accompany us in the hope of doing some biological work among the spruce forests of the Coppermine Valley.

February 2 arrived, the date set for our departure. About 8 A. M. a bluish tinge began to creep over the snow. It grew perceptibly brighter until we could distinguish the dark shore-line of the harbour, and the island that barred the entrance. In the distance the Liston and Sutton Islands appeared as a thin black

[ 63 ]

line raised by the mirage a few inches above the horizon. The air was calm and clear, the temperature comparatively mild, with the thermometer registering only —12° F. Everything seemed to promise fine travelling weather as we set about harnessing the dogs.

There were two toboggans in our outfit, besides the sled and dog-team of five that I had used throughout the winter. One toboggan, drawn by six of the expedition's best dogs, was for Anderson and his companion; the other, with seven dogs, for Johansen. We distributed our loads at the outset in the proportion of a hundred pounds for each dog, but they naturally became lighter every day we travelled. One of our tents had the ordinary A shape; the other, for Anderson's use, resembled a domed beehive, being modelled on the tents used by Eskimos and Indians in the north of Alaska. We carried two stoves for wood and two others for oil, since we might not find wood at every spot we camped. The rest of our baggage consisted of dog-food and man-food, sleeping-gear and bags of spare clothing. A rifle and a pair of snow-shoes for each man lay ready to hand on top of the loads, directly under the lashings.

The weather remained fine for the first week, and our daily run averaged about fifteen miles. We passed under Cape Lambert on the second day; its cliffs of cherty dolomite, rising to a height of eighty feet and extending for about a mile along the coast, appeared as a notable landmark in the otherwise featureless shore-line. Farther east was a low stone monument set up by Sir John Richardson's party nearly seventy years before, although from its appearance it might have been standing but a few months. Time's ravages work slowly in the Arctic; M'Clintock's expedition to Melville Island in 1853 discovered hardly a trace of moss on the tracks of Sir Edward Parry's carts that had passed over the tundra in 1820.

We encountered our first caribou in Richardson Bay, near the mouth of the Coppermine River, where a herd of about a hundred were grazing on a ridge overlooking the frozen sea. Anderson and Palaiyak pursued them and shot three. We cached part of the meat under the largest boulders we could find; but since the wolverines would dislodge a stone that two of us could hardly lift, we covered the boulders with snow, and converted the snow into ice by pouring water over it. We hoped by this means to outwit the crafty animals and preserve a small stock of meat for Anderson's return journey. But they proved too much for us; they tunnelled under the surrounding snow and entered the cache from below, as we discovered a fortnight later.

Every hunter in the North develops a taste for the marrow in the leg-bones of the caribou; so it was not surprising that Anderson, Johansen, and myself, sitting round the camp-stove that night, should pile two dozen bones in our midst, and proceed to crack them on stone anvils with our hunting-knives. Anderson then became strangely reminiscent, and related droll stories of his college days, of the Spanish-American War, and of his experiences on a former expedition to the Arctic. Suddenly he stopped, and Johansen and I returned to the marrow-bones. Nothing remained but fragments. I could account for four bones only, Johansen for only two; Anderson himself had slyly demolished the other eighteen. In fairness, however, I should add that he has always denied the accuracy of these figures.

The long, winding Coppermine enters the sea by two mouths, which are separated from one another by a low, grass-covered island capped with two diabase hills at its northern end. The river is here about three miles wide, but immediately narrows down to a few hundred yards. We encountered nothing but smooth ice for the first ten miles, so smooth that the snow had blown off it in many places. The dogs soon lost their tempers here, for they slid over the ice in all directions when the toboggans stuck fast on the tiniest snow-patch. Steep mud-banks hemmed us in on either side, sloping back to a level plateau in a series of cone-shaped pyramids. We came upon willows growing as high as seven or eight feet, the nearest approach to trees that any of us had seen for many months; and we passed two deserted snow-houses erected by some Eskimos returning from the Dismal Lakes early in the winter. Just as darkness began to close in we pitched our tent three miles from Bloody Fall, where Hearne, the first white man to behold the northern ocean, witnessed the massacre of a whole community of Eskimos by his bloodthirsty bodyguard of Chipewyan Indians.

We, too, had an adventure in this tragic spot, an adventure that savoured of comedy, although it appeared serious enough at the moment. While we were dressing in the morning a tumult arose among the dogs, and Johansen pushed open the flap of the tent to investigate. "Come quickly," he cried; "a big wolf is chewing up the dogs"; and he dashed out to rescue his favourite team leader. We followed, clad only in short breeks and sealskin slippers. The wolf sneaked in front of my sled not ten yards from me, and our rifles lay beyond it. I hurled a large boulder at its head, but it leaped aside, and tried to bury its fangs in my naked leg. I held it off like a dog, gripping the nape of its neck; and it twisted its head around and caught my forearm. Then I tried to throttle it with my left hand, cave-man fashion; but the animal would have mauled me badly, I fear, had it not voluntarily released its grip and slunk away, only to fall from Anderson's bullet. As it was I escaped with a small flesh-wound that, thanks to the germ-free atmosphere of the North, healed almost entirely within a week.

Owing to this accident Anderson decided not to break camp that day, but to utilize the time in caching some of the provisions. Palaiyak went out to hunt caribou. He returned in the evening empty-handed, but reported a curious experience exactly like one that had occurred to Sir John Richardson in this neighbourhood. While stalking a herd late in the afternoon Palaiyak noticed five wolves in front of him engaged in the same pursuit. One wolf kept far over to the flank; the others, in horseshoe formation, were driving the herd toward a distant cliff. The animals moved away from him so rapidly that he did not see the issue; but if we had troubled to search in the morning we should probably have found the mangled bones of the caribou at the foot of the cliff, and foxes devouring the last shreds left by the wolves.

Bloody Fall, below which we camped, is a dangerous rapid where the Coppermine River cuts through a dyke of hard diabase rock running parallel to the coast-line. The swift current keeps the river open in the severest winter, but the traveller can usually pass through the gorge on the ice-foot that forms under its western bank. About the fall the ice was piled up in broken masses, and lanes of open water here and there made it impossible to follow the river channel with sled and dog-team. We, therefore, crossed over to the right bank and climbed onto the plateau, where the soft, deep snow compelled us to put on our snow-shoes. Anderson gave a whoop of joy and leaped four feet into the air when he felt the familiar straps around his ankles; but the dogs floundered up to their bellies at every step, and buried their tails between their legs as they wearily dragged the toboggans up and down the ridges.

Two days of this travelling brought us to a grove of medium-sized spruce trees in the sheltered valley of a small stream not far from the Sandstone Rapids. We were then about forty miles from the mouth of the Coppermine, and a hundred and thirty from Bernard Harbour. The north-east corner of Great Bear Lake was less than a hundred miles away, and if Anderson once reached the lake the worst part of his journey would be over, even though Fort Norman lay twice as far beyond. Johansen's goal was the forest in which we had now camped, so he and his toboggan would go no farther.

We lingered a day near the Sandstone Rapids to reorganize the loads and repair a tent that the dogs had torn. Anderson, Castel, and I then pushed on ten miles to another grove of spruce trees surrounding a tiny lagoon. The Coppermine was half a mile to the westward, and the Kendall River flowing out of the Dismal Lakes entered on the opposite bank. We tried hard to reach it before dark; but three steep ridges separated the lagoon from the Coppermine, and Anderson's heavy toboggan failed to surmount the first of them, though I carried three hundred pounds of his load on my sled. He decided to camp in the grove for the night and renew the attempt next day, freighting his supplies in two relays. When I left them in the morning he was confident of crossing the river before noon; but so steep were the ridges, and so deep the snow, that they laboured for two days before reaching the nearer bank.

Meanwhile, at our old camp in the first grove of spruce trees, Johansen was greatly elated by an unexpected discovery. He told me, when I returned, that he had solved a problem that had baffled every traveller on the Coppermine from the days of Richardson to our own. East and west of the river stretch the barren grounds, stony or mossy, according to the varying conditions, but nowhere adorned by a single tree except the creeping dwarf willow. The tree-line follows the valleys, and on the larger rivers runs nearly out to the coast. On the Coppermine the most northerly stand of timber lies in the valley of a small creek six miles from the sea and three or four miles from the actual river-bed; south of this, groves of spruce, mingled with a little cottonwood, appear at intervals of every mile or two, the groves becoming larger, and the trees bigger, as one travels upstream. All the bigger trees in the northernmost groves are dead, and many of the smaller ones have dead and withered branches, so that the timber-line seems to be moving southward. Richardson attributed this movement to fires kindled by wandering bands of Eskimos, but the botanists were never quite satisfied with his explanation. Johansen now offered a different one. By cutting into the trees he had discovered many dead beetles and their larvæ, even a larva still living. Three or four genera were represented, all known to be a menace to our northern forests, since they sap the strength of the larger branches. The beetles had themselves been killed by abnormally cold weather; but it seemed certain that they, and not fires, were responsible for the destruction of the timber and the recession of the tree-line. Johansen had good reason to be elated at his discovery.

We stayed two days longer in the grove to enable him to continue his researches. Palaiyak went caribou-hunting, for three men and twelve dogs will consume a whole carcass in one day. I spent most of the time cooking the meals, attending to the dogs, and performing the other routine duties incident to camp life. The temperature had fallen as soon as we left the coast, and our mercury thermometer froze at —51° F.; but the atmosphere was calm and dry, and the cold caused us little inconvenience. A brilliant display of parhelia illumined the dark spruce trees that rose straight out of the white snow, and the landscape was surprisingly beautiful after the barren monotony of the sea-coast.

The second afternoon I wandered down to the river to watch the clouds of vapour steaming up from the open water, and as I passed through the grove I caught a glimpse of Johansen, poised on snow-shoes, hewing with all his might at one of the largest trees in the vicinity. His hands so tingled with the cold that he often dropped the axe to clap them vigorously against one another or to thaw them inside his fur breeches. But he was whistling cheerfully, willing to lose his fingers rather than forsake his precious beetles.

Palaiyak reported an abundance of game in the vicinity of our camp; during a single day's hunting he saw two hundred caribou, a wolverine, a red fox, and the tracks of many wolves. We had warned him not to shoot more caribou than we could eat or carry with us on our sleds, and he limited himself to three; but he brought in also two large hares that made a fine mulligan stew.

As soon as Johansen had collected enough specimens we broke camp and started back toward the coast. The sled and toboggan were piled high with meat, but the dogs pulled cheerfully along their old trail, knowing as well as we did that it led to Bernard Harbour. We were looking for no adventures down the river, and experienced none, unless it were the trifling mishap that befell us near Bloody Fall.

I have called it a mishap, but Johansen would say a disaster. I was in front, breaking trail up a long ridge. Just as I reached the crest a large herd of caribou began to straggle unconcernedly across our path almost within reach of a shotgun. We had all the meat that we could carry, and did not wish to alarm them needlessly; so I cowed my excited dogs into quiescence, and stationed Palaiyak at the handle-bars of the sled to check a run-away. Neither of us thought of Johansen, who plodded wearily behind on his snow-shoes, noticing nothing. But when his team sighted the herd it dashed away so suddenly that the astonished driver had no time even to throw himself on top of the toboggan. The caribou fled; the dogs pursued them, Johansen pursued the dogs, and I watched the stampede through the binoculars. The herd disappeared at last over a distant ridge, and the dogs, losing all zest for a chase where the quarry was no longer in sight, stretched out their panting bodies on the snow and awaited the wrathful Johansen. He wheeled them round and led them back to the trail, their heads drooping penitently, and their tails trailing between their legs. No one ventured a word as the doleful procession drew near; we silently banished the incident into the storehouse of memory and resumed our interrupted march.

It seemed strange to us then that the Coppermine Eskimos did not hunt these caribou during the winter months, instead of watching for hours over the breath-ing-holes of seals, exposed to every gale that swept the level ice-fields. When we questioned some of them a few days later, they explained that the intense cold inland would snap the lashings of their bows. This was not true, for other Eskimos who possessed no weapons except bows and arrows before the introduction of rifles hunted in the interior all through the winter. But these inland Eskimos used caribou fat in their stone lamps, and caribou fat is a miserable substitute for seal-blubber, which gives a far purer and hotter flame. There lay the real explanation. The Coppermine Eskimos could have hunted the caribou if they wished, but they preferred the sea-ice and its more comfortable homes lit up by the burning blubber.

The temperature was only —30° F., 20° higher than inland, when we reached the mouth of the Coppermine; yet the cold seemed more biting, for the air was damp, the atmosphere foggy, and a slight northeast wind blew directly in our faces. We struck out northward over the ice, and on the second day sighted three Eskimos standing over their seal-holes. They viewed with alarm the strange sled and toboggan, so different from any of their own; but our peace-signal banished their fears, and they joyfully guided us to their village a few miles farther on. The whole population turned out to welcome us and to assist in setting up our tent, which they seemed to understand almost as well as ourselves. They understood, also, our stove for burning wood, for they informed us that there was no driftwood within five miles of their settlement and offered to lend us two stone lamps and a little blubber.

In these and other ways they showed a greater
familiarity with the customs of the white man than
the natives of Dolphin and Union Strait. We found
even more astounding evidences of contact with Euro-
peans when we visited their snow-huts.

The village itself differed slightly from the usual
type, the houses being arranged in line and separated
by considerable intervals; normally they lie in a cluster,
in order that no evil spirits may harm the inmates as
they wander in the darkness from one hut to another.
Johansen and I began our tour at one end, and dropped
a trail of matches and needles along the line to show
our appreciation of the scraps of blubber, meat, and
fish with which each housewife paid us tribute. The
last hut was also the largest. A dance-house framed
the entrance, and half a dozen dogs, twice the usual
number, squabbled in the passage, indicating that the
occupant was a man of influence in his community. We
brushed the dogs aside, and crawled on hands and
knees through the low doorway at the inner end.
Seated in state on his sleeping-platform was Knife,
by repute the shrewdest Eskimo, and the most powerful medicine-man, in this section of the country; and
on each side of him, supporting his dignity, sat a wife,
the one chosen for her beauty, the other for her skill
in hunting. He smiled a welcome as we entered, and,
with a haughty gesture of his hand, motioned the
younger woman to give us her seat.

We lingered a few minutes only, but I visited him again in the evening, when he had the stage all set for my reception. The hut was thronged with hunters sipping oily tea from two small china cups. Over the blubber-lamp hung an iron cauldron from which Knife dipped up the evil-looking beverage with a greasy ladle of musk-ox horn. Some of his treasures lay beside him, dragged out of bags and boxes for my edification. There were two rifles, a Hollis double-barrelled fowling-piece, a pipe, plug tobacco, and part of an American magazine; strangest of all, a Roman breviary and an illustrated French Scripture book.

How, and where, had he obtained these last? Hanbury, the English explorer who passed through this country twelve years before, had certainly not carried them on his sled. Captain Bernard might have brought some of them on his vessel when he wintered in 1910 near the mouth of the Coppermine River; but surely he had no Roman breviary or French Scripture book? How did they come into the possession of the Eskimos?

I questioned Knife. The previous summer, he said, he and his kinsmen had traded with three white men near Great Bear Lake. One of the white men, who wore a robe and a crucifix, was especially friendly, and when Knife and his companions secured him a supply of fresh meat, rewarded them with many presents, among them the rifles and the books.

Knife's answer seemed plausible enough at the moment, and I made no further enquiries. Later I began to doubt his story, for what priest would give his Latin breviary to a savage? Palaiyak then told me, too, that he had seen a cassock and a crucifix in another hut. There must have been foul play somewhere. Had the Eskimos robbed the missionary? Had they murdered him?

I questioned Knife again a few weeks later, but he merely repeated the same story. A corporal of the Royal Northwest Mounted Police attached himself to our party the next autumn, and the following spring an inspector brought in a patrol from Great Bear Lake. Then the grim story came gradually to light.

*　　*　　*

Two French missionaries, Fathers Rouvier and LeRoux, passed through Great Bear Lake in the summer of 1912, charged with the establishment of a mission among the pagan inhabitants of Coronation Gulf. They began their ministrations on the Dismal Lakes, whither a few Eskimo families drifted in search of caribou; but the Eskimos vanished to the northward with the coming of the first snows, and the priests were left in solitude all winter. The natives visited them again the following summer, and the priests, determined not to lose sight of them, accompanied them to the coast. Trouble arose almost immediately. The

Eskimo with whom they lodged coveted one of their rifles, and became openly hostile when they refused to part with it. His kinsmen supported him; other natives took the side of the two missionaries, and the camp was divided against itself. One of the elder men advised the missionaries to depart; he lent them one of his dogs, helped to load up their sled, and himself escorted them for the first two miles until the danger seemed over. Then he returned to the settlement, and the priests continued their way alone up the Coppermine River.

Two hunters who left the settlement the next day followed their trail up the river. Years later they declared that they went to help some kinsmen who had not yet descended to the coast. Whatever their real purpose, they overtook the priests not far from the ill-omened Bloody Fall, and agreed to haul their sled as far as the first timber in return for a few fox-traps. All day they pulled ahead of the dogs, and at evening built two snow-houses, one for themselves and one for the priests. Both parties spent the night in misery, for their clothing was damp with perspiration, and they had no fuel to mitigate the intense cold. They struggled ahead in the morning in the face of a blinding snow-storm, which drove them out of their course. The Eskimos, not accustomed to work for others and weary of the heavy hauling, wanted to abandon the priests; but the latter dared not let them depart,

[ 78 ]

knowing that without aid they themselves could never reach the timber. One priest went in front to break the trail, the other marched behind the sled, threatening the natives with his rifle whenever they halted or turned back. The terrified Eskimos plotted to kill them and watched for an opportunity. When the priest behind them slackened his guard for a moment they leaped upon him with their knives, stabbed him to death, and shot his companion with the rifle. Then they cut open the bodies of their victims and ate the livers, a gruesome custom general among nearly all Eskimo tribes to render the spirits of the dead innocuous.

The hunters now returned and reported their crime to the people at the mouth of the river, who ascended to the scene of the murders and plundered the sled. Knife was not present on this occasion, but the following summer, while we were establishing our base at Bernard Harbour, he and his kinsmen pillaged the missionaries' cabin at the Dismal Lakes. Several Eskimos in this village that Johansen and I were visiting held property belonging to the priests, and the ringleader of the two murderers actually entertained us in his house. Strangely enough, we were greatly impressed by his bearing, and considered him one of the most enterprising and reliable natives that we had yet encountered.

Police arrested the two murderers about eighteen

months after my visit and carried them south for trial.
Both men were sentenced to death, but the penalty
was later commuted to two years' imprisonment. They
were ultimately restored to their homes, where one of
them, profiting by his experience of civilization, rendered useful service to the new police posts that were
established in Coronation Gulf.

The news that white men were wintering in their
country not eighty miles away caused a great commo-
tion among the villagers. They anticipated a renewal
of their profitable trade with Captain Bernard four
years before, and hastily prepared to migrate en
masse to Bernard Harbour. Before dawn a long file
of sleds, laden five and six feet high with the family
possessions, streamed slowly over the snow in the
direction of Locker Point. Wives and daughters pulled
in front of the dogs, urging them on with frequent
cries; fathers and sons hauled behind them, giving added
encouragement with their walking-sticks. Here an old
woman staggered feebly along, clutching the sled for
support; there a dog running loose dragged an old man
at the end of its trace. A nine-months-old baby slept
peacefully on top of a load, enveloped in a caribou skin
to protect it from the wind. Far in the rear came
Knife's big sled, loaded to its full capacity, and trailing
a smaller sled laden almost as heavily. Wealth has its
disadvantages in the Arctic also; Knife could hardly

transport all his property even with two wives and six dogs.

The natives travelled sixteen miles before they unhitched their teams and built new snow-houses for the night. The men went sealing the next morning, for at this season of the year they rarely had food for more than three days, and could travel long distances only in stages. Elated with the number of seals they captured they moved on the following morning, although the temperature was —29° F., and a howling north-west gale lashed their faces with hard snow. Johansen and I put on masks to protect our cheeks and noses, but discarded them before noon when the thick layer of frost that formed on their inside began to cling to our chins. Many of the Eskimos had their cheeks frozen, still more their wrists, for their short travelling mittens left an uncovered space between the hands and the coat-sleeves. Yet in the height of the storm a woman crouched down in the lee of her sled, withdrew a tiny baby from under her jacket and leisurely changed its sole garment, a diaper of caribou fur. The baby suffered no harm, apparently; but children were not always so fortunate, and the infant mortality was terribly high.

We had no intention of letting this horde of more than a hundred natives break in upon the tranquillity of Bernard Harbour without due warning. Our dogs

travelled faster than theirs, and our tent did away
with the necessity of halting before dark to build a
snow-hut. We pushed ahead of all the sleds and
camped eight miles beyond them at Cape Lambert.
One long day's march then brought us to our station
on March 1, the exact date pre-arranged for our return. The vanguard of the Eskimos did not appear
until twenty-four hours later, by which time we had
made preparations for their reception.

# CHAPTER VI

## LENGTHENING DAYS

**B**ERNARD HARBOUR presented a scene of extraordinary activity and confusion during the three weeks following our return; in fact, it was the busiest and most populous trading post in the whole of Arctic Canada. Five-score natives were living in snow-huts along the beach not fifty yards from our door; and from a similar settlement a few miles away men, women, and even children drifted across daily to trade with us and to visit our neighbours. We tried to bar them from the house during the day and let them enter after supper only; but they flooded in at all hours, and treated the place exactly like one of their own homes.

I myself was glad of their presence. I could spend

the whole day inside our warm house writing down their customs and beliefs; and I could buy all the specimens they offered me, for the tents where I stored them lay right at our door. The natives sang dance-songs each evening into my phonograph, and helped to transcribe the words when I played them over for their entertainment. True, their numbers embarrassed me occasionally; they jostled my arm as they crowded around, talked incessantly all at the same time, and laughed at the babel of their own voices. But they were always good-natured, and genuinely interested in helping on my work.

The other four residents of our little home hardly welcomed the intrusion, although they cheerfully endured it from a misguided compassion for me. They usually took refuge in their bunks after supper, to delve into Arctic literature or ponder over scientific notes; but whenever the invasion threatened to overwhelm me, they came to the rescue by delivering an attack on the flanks. O'Neill displayed queer conjuring tricks, Johansen showed pictures of strange birds and animals, Chipman drew the likenesses of our visitors, and Cox made them join hands and dip for trinkets into a bowl of salt water connected with two or three electric cells. The natives turned the tables on us one evening by subjecting our faces to a rigid scrutiny. Chipman and O'Neill, they concluded, were very young because they seemed to grow no beards, but

Johansen, who wore an imperial, and I, who trimmed my beard once a week with a pair of No. o clippers, were quite elderly. They asked me at last whether the two former were not my sons. I gravely assured them they were not mine, but Johansen's.

Nothing disturbed the harmony of our relations until some natives from the settlement near the Liston and Sutton Islands reported that one of their young men had died a short time before, and openly accused me of his murder. They could not charge me with physical violence, for I was a hundred miles away on the Coppermine River at the time of his decease; but they said that I had stolen his soul by magic, and deliberately withheld it until his body pined away and died. Foolish as this accusation seemed, we could not blind ourselves to its seriousness. The Eskimos knew nothing of our law or of the police. Their own penalty for murder was assassination, unless the relatives of the dead man agreed to accept a heavy blood-price. They might not have dared to apply this penalty to me, because trading would cease immediately and my well-armed party make reprisals. But no one could say what would happen. Certainly it was not safe for me to wander in and out of their huts as freely as before; some hot-headed individual might forget discretion and stab me in the back as I crawled through a low doorway.

In spite of the preponderating sentiment against

me, a few of my Eskimo friends still believed in my innocence, and sought for an influential medicine-man who could unravel the mystery of the young man's death. Knife's arrival was well timed, for no medicine-man in the district enjoyed greater prestige. The familiar spirits of which he was the mouthpiece spoke infallible truth, and whether they pronounced me innocent or guilty the verdict would carry credence everywhere.

Palaiyak returned from the snow-huts on the beach one evening and whispered in my ear that Knife was in the dance-house preparing to hold his investigation. I calculated the chances quickly. Knife knew that I spoke his language, and it was not in Eskimo nature to accuse a man of murder to his face. Moreover he was crafty, and would consult his own interests before everything else. At the present moment he sorely needed ammunition and other goods that I could supply. Would he dare to name me guilty to my face? I decided to attend his séance and hear the verdict myself.

The people had ceased dancing when I entered the hut and were whiling away the moments by singing without the drum. Half of them were drawn up in a circle; the remainder, for whom there was no room in the ring, formed knots of two and three in the background. Over in one corner stood Cockney, our English cook, who had been quietly watching the performances. He did not know that I was accused of murder, or that anything more was in progress than an ordinary dance, and it seemed wiser not to enlighten him. Knife himself sat on the sleeping-platform, paying no heed to what went on around him; but he glanced at me furtively when I entered and looked a trifle disconcerted.

The singing continued but a few minutes longer, when the impatient audience entreated Knife to summon his familiar spirits. He sat now with closed eyes, half dozing as it seemed. Suddenly he gasped, choking cries burst from his lips, and, staggering into the centre of the ring, he motioned me to stand near him. A quiver passed over the audience; at last the truth of the murder would be revealed. The choking cries gave place to wild gibberish, which his father, standing beside me, interpreted as the language of white men. Knife, less hysterical than he appeared, heard the old man's words, and, staring straight into my face, repeated his gibberish. *"Quadrupedante putrem sonitu quatit ungula campum,"* I answered immediately in the first words of Latin that came into my head; and *"pamakalawilinilitoolooka,"* or something like it, he responded in his gibberish. My Latin gave out, and I continued the conversation in French, fearing to use English lest Cockney might ruin the little drama by some false move. The impression on the audience was immense; their shaman really was inspired by a

white man's spirit, for how else could he understand
and converse with me? So when he ceased his gibberish, and in broken syllables pronounced that it was
a white man in a far distant country who had caused
the young man's death, the faith that moves mountains
was not stronger than their conviction of my innocence.

All this time Cockney had been viewing our antics
with the greatest alarm. Knife held me hypnotized,
he believed, and the tense faces of the audience turned
in my direction made him dread some untoward incident. He dared not abandon me to my peril while he
warned our companions at the house above. So he
stood, like a vigilant sentry, prepared to leap to my
rescue and battle against the overwhelming odds the
moment the whistle sounded.

The séance lasted about two hours, and contained
several minor incidents in which I played a leading rôle.
Knife's audience was in the mood to credit any decep-
tion, and he was too shrewd to lose his opportunity.
At one stage he led his first wife into the ring to exe-
cute a "white man's" reel, a kind of square dance they
had learned at Great Bear Lake; and in his wild gibberish, made intelligible to me by signs, he bade me
summon Cockney to join hands with the younger wife.
The dance may not have been artistic, but it impressed
the spectators more than ever with the wondrous
knowledge of their medicine-man, who could both

speak the white man's language and perform his intricate dances.

The performance ended at last, and the people began to disperse to their huts. Cockney, who was among the first to vanish, hastened to the station to describe my abnormal behaviour and organize a strong party that would bring me safely home. But before he had finished his narrative I myself arrived on the scene and offered a more reasonable explanation of my conduct.

The natives living out in the strait became very friendly again when the charge of murder was lifted from my head. I visited their settlement twice for periods of three or four days, staying each time with my old acquaintance, Ikpuck. The sun was now much higher in the sky, and a mildness in the atmosphere indicated the approach of spring. Snow-huts would soon be untenable; the slight melting of their ceilings around noon had already caused some of the people to move into large tents made of caribou skins. With the advent of longer days the hunters captured more seals, and the women were packing the surplus blubber into large bags to cache on the coast until autumn. Everything seemed to be changing. The various bands that had united in midwinter were separating out again and moving to different sealing-grounds; and every fortnight, as the new sealing-grounds became exhausted, they moved their settlements forward a few more miles. Even the little children had work to do, for this harvest season would last only until May, when the breaking up of the sea-ice would drive the natives from their sealing to fish and hunt caribou on the land.

It was time now to decide what my own movements should be during the summer months, and I suggested to Ikpuck that I might join his train to Victoria Island, taking my own outfit. The old man was delighted with the plan, and, having no children of his own, formally adopted me into his family, which consisted of himself and his wife Icehouse, Sculpin or Jennie, Icehouse's daughter by a former marriage, and an adopted nephew named Knife-Blade. The Runner, a married son of Icehouse, intended to join the party; probably also two or three families of near kinsmen. The entire band would assemble on the ice within the next three or four weeks, when Ikpuck would send word to me at the station. In the meantime I could travel east with Cox, who needed a companion and a dog-team for surveying a portion of the coast-line.

The short trip with Cox was a pleasant change from constant association with the Eskimos; it was like moving from one world into another. Yet we could not avoid the natives entirely. Two families were hunting large bearded seals in a bay a few miles east of our station, and a small band had camped near Cape

Krusenstern to intercept the herds of caribou that were now migrating northward from their winter home on the Barren Lands. Both these camps we passed without stopping, glad that the few logs of driftwood along the coast made it necessary to seek their blubber-lamps for drying our boots and mittens. The wood petered out just beyond Cape Krusenstern, and we did lodge one night in a native's tent; but when Cox tried to take observations outside for latitude and longitude, his sextant and artificial horizon attracted so many curious observers that he seldom caught a glimpse of the sun. The long-suffering topographer finally became so ruffled that we hastily left the settlement and camped seven miles away beside a large log of cottonwood that provided enough fuel for three days.

Hardly had we pitched our tent when a sled appeared coming up from the south. The travellers were Anderson and Castel, returning from their unsuccessful attempt to reach Fort Norman. With infinite labour they had struggled through deep snow from the valley of the Coppermine to Dease River. There Anderson had expected to find white men, or at least Indians working for them, who would carry the mail to Fort Norman before the ice broke up; but the country was deserted. The winter was then so advanced that if he pushed on to Fort Norman he could not return to Bernard Harbour in time to organize our scientific work for the spring and summer. He decided, therefore, to turn back and forward the mail by ship when the season for navigation arrived.

With the extra man and dog-team now available, Cox no longer required my assistance in his topographical work; so we returned to the station with Anderson to arrange the programs for the next seven months. Cox intended to complete the map of the coast-line to the mouth of the Rae River, then, ascending the river to its source, cross overland to Bernard Harbour. Chipman and O'Neill would finish their survey of the western coast-line to Darnley Bay; afterward they would continue Cox's survey, extending it from the mouth of the Rae River to the eastern end of Coronation Gulf, where Cox and Anderson would join them in our schooner, the *North Star,* as soon as the ice broke up. Anderson and Johansen were to carry on biological and zoological work at the station during the spring, and Johansen would remain there all summer after Anderson went eastward. I myself proposed to join the Eskimos going to Victoria Island, and return to Bernard Harbour when the sea froze over again in November. Each man worked out his own plans to harmonize with the rest, and Anderson, with full confidence in his staff, approved them all without question, seeking only ways and means to furnish the necessary equipment.

My "father" Ikpuck arrived four days later to guide me to his settlement, which had been moved twice during my brief absence. It was now mid-April, and the natives were travelling in easy stages toward the land, allowing a few days between each migration for the women and children to freight forward the pokes of blubber and the men to resume their sealing. All the families had adopted skin tents in place of snow-houses, or, if their tents were still cached on the coast, they roofed circular walls of snow with the skins of caribou and musk-oxen. The camp was mottled with clothing, suspended from sticks, to dry in the warm sun; and at every little snow-flurry the women rushed from the tents to beat the light flakes from each garment before they melted and spoiled the fur. Night and day had merged into one another, the sun disappearing for one hour only at midnight; and the temperature remained fairly constant around 15°F., except at noon, when it mounted at times to the freezing-point.

The younger women, who were as well versed as the men in the peculiar habits of the seal, often went out with the hunters to escape the monotonous care of clothes and blubber. Each seal appeared to have its special territory, like a bird in the nesting season; and every half-hour or so it came to the surface to breathe. In summer, with open water all around, it rose at any place; but when the sea froze in the autumn it could reach the atmosphere only by breaking through the thin sheet of ice that covered its domain. The breathing-holes made at that season remained open all winter, for the snow that drifted over them, mantling the whole ice-field, kept them from freezing beyond the power of the animal to break through at its next visit. The seal then remained in this territory, making irregular circuits from one hole to another.

The Eskimo adjusted his hunting to the animal's habits. When his well-trained dog, nosing over the surface, scented the taint of a seal-hole and vigorously scratched up the snow, he drove it back and himself cleared out the cavity with a small scoop. Then from the back of his coat he brought forth an "indicator," a thin stick of bone that resembled a knitting-needle with a small disc near the lower end. He arranged this to float upright in the water, and adjusted the snow around the top until the opening was scarcely visible. Everything was now ready, and, harpoon in hand, he crouched on the lee side of the hole to await his quarry. Sometimes it appeared within a few minutes; sometimes, when it was visiting other holes in the circuit, not for several hours. But when the indicator bobbed rapidly up and down with the air-bubbles he knew that the seal was rising to the surface; and when the indicator jerked suddenly upward he drove his harpoon down through the centre of the hole and clung to the line with all his might.

The days passed pleasantly by. As a member of Ikpuck's household I occupied one edge of his sleep-ing-platform and stored my supplies on the snow wall that encircled his tent. My dogs made friends with his dogs, and shared the same home in the passageway. Jennie, my eleven-year-old "sister," took charge of them during migrations while I hauled on the big sled with Ikpuck. The other families in the band considered me a guest of distinction and welcomed me into their homes. So little by little civilization slipped from me and I settled down to the routine of Eskimo life.

Ikpuck asked me one morning to accompany him westward to bring back some caribou fat he had cached on the coast the previous summer. I understood that the whole trip would occupy only two or three days; but, to avoid all risks, I put together provisions for four. We started out the same morning, Ikpuck running ahead of the sled to give the course. By evening we had travelled over twenty-five miles, and were still as far out from shore as when we started. I discovered then the actual length of the journey; it would take two or three days merely to reach the cache, and at least the same number to return.

We covered about thirty miles the next day and camped behind Cape Kendall, on Victoria Island. Ikpuck remarked as we turned into our sleeping-bags that we should reach the cache in the morning, and return to our camp at night. After tossing restlessly in bed for several hours from the pain of snow-blindness—for travelling through broken ice causes a heavy strain on the eyes, particularly when the weather is foggy—I fell at last into a sound sleep and did not awaken until 7 o'clock in the morning. Ikpuck had disappeared, even the dogs and sled were gone. I was alone in an empty snow-hut, without food and crippled with snow-blindness, eighty miles from Bernard Harbour. The thought flashed through my mind that Ikpuck had deliberately abandoned me to gain possession of my outfit, and, stumbling outside, I followed his tracks for a few yards; but they led to the westward, in the direction, not of his settlement, but of the cache. I entered the house again, and, looking around, saw in a corner some rice that had been left over from our supper, and a piece of frozen seal meat that Ikpuck had brought in from the sled before he departed. Then I felt ashamed of my suspicions. The faithful old man had left me to sleep while he went on alone to his cache; and he would join me again within a few hours.

I lay all day in my sleeping-bag, shielding my eyes from the light; and the inflammation abated so rapidly with the darkness and rest that I could probably travel the next day without much discomfort. Ikpuck appeared late in the evening, his sled loaded up to the handle-bars with caribou fat. A broad smile lit up his face as he spoke of the trick he had played me. "You were tired last night," he said, "and your eyes were bloodshot and painful. I should have returned much earlier, but the dogs were troublesome and the load heavier than I anticipated."

I questioned him about his route, for the two maps on which I relied, that of Rae, the Arctic explorer, and the chart of the British Admiralty, disagreed concerning this part of the coast. The chart had a deep inlet behind Cape Kendall which did not appear on Rae's map, while Rae (who named the cape Point Pullen) showed an island to the westward that was missing on the chart. Ikpuck's explanation, and my own observations later in the summer, revealed a land-locked bay that nearly severed Cape Kendall from the mainland; in portaging across the isthmus instead of following the coast, Ikpuck had shortened his journey by several miles. West of the point a long sandbar stretched out toward a high, rocky islet that harboured the remains of an ancient settlement. Both maps, then, were right; the full truth lay in combining them.

Our load of caribou fat was indeed heavy, for it had been lying in a cache eight months. It weighted not only the sled, but the surrounding atmosphere. I kept to windward of it, or well in front of the dogs, but distance seemed to make no appreciable difference. Ikpuck, on the contrary, sniffed the air with satisfaction, and nibbled small pieces of the fat as we marched along. When the provisions we had brought gave out that evening it furnished him both breakfast and supper. Only thirst distressed him, for we had exhausted the oil in our primus lamp and had no means of melting ice or snow. Fortunately, thirty-six hours later, we came upon a settlement of four snow-huts occupied by some Eskimos who were migrating to the mainland, and were able to slake our thirst from their cooking-pots. These natives, too, seemed to regard our caribou fat as an unusual luxury; but I myself derived more enjoyment from the juicy meat of a freshly killed seal.

The distance from this settlement to our own was only about fifteen miles, which we expected to cover easily in one day; but a heavy fall of snow at night obliterated all the trails, and the dense fog that succeeded hid from view everything beyond the leading dog. We wandered from early morning until late in the evening vainly searching for the tents, and at last, giving up all hope, built a small snow-hut and turned into our sleeping-bags. I filled a cup with snow to thaw out against my body, and realized, as never before, how much heat is required to melt a little snow, and how much snow to yield one teaspoonful of water.

The fog dispersed before morning, and we discovered the settlement a mile and a half to our left. An hour later Icehouse was distributing the caribou fat among the enthusiastic villagers, while Ikpuck and I, resting on the sleeping-platform, regaled ourselves with seal meat and hot tea. So ended our little journey, which began as a pleasant excursion, but developed, for me at least, into a rather toilsome march. Ikpuck was more accustomed to such vicissitudes, and thought the incident hardly worth mentioning.

We lingered a fortnight longer on the sea-ice, revelling in the mild weather of the Arctic spring. Day and night were hardly distinguishable, for the end of April saw the midnight sun. It mattered little whether we retired to our sleeping-bags at midnight or at noon; the night hours were preferable for travelling, because by 7 P.M. the melting slush of noon began to freeze again and the heavily laden sleds glided along more easily. When the days were warm and sunny a few seals emerged from their holes to bask on the surface of the ice, and in clear weather one or two herds of caribou marched steadily past us toward Victoria Island.

Slowly we too moved northward, travelling about twelve miles at a time, then halting for a week to allow the hunters to capture a few more seals, and their wives to accumulate more blubber. During one of these journeys my companions discovered a seal-hole covered as usual by the crust of snow. I thought it was nothing but the ordinary breathing-hole, about a foot in diameter, leading down to the water, and was lingering beside my sled, when Ikpuck called me over to examine it. Burrowed out in the snow alongside the hole was a small oval chamber where the seal had given birth to its pup two months before and nourished it during the first days of its existence. How long the young seal remained in this chamber before it followed its mother into the water, and whether it

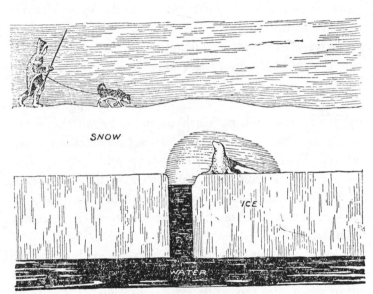

ever returned there to rest after its long swims, I do not know. A white man would have walked over its home and detected nothing. When my companions pointed out to me the peculiar convexity of the crust which had first attracted their attention, my untrained eyes could hardly distinguish it from a score of similar inequalities within the radius of a quarter of a mile.

[ 100 ]

The Eskimos, who were greatly amused at my ignorance of everything pertaining to sealing, now scored another laugh at my expense. As we gazed down into the seal-hole one of them asked me whether I intended to drink from it. The joke seemed so obvious that I answered rather casually, "No. I do not care to drink salt sea-water." But the men around me smiled, and my questioner, kneeling down, scooped up a handful of slush ice that was floating on the surface, let it drain through his fingers for a moment, and swallowed it with gusto. Still doubting, I tested the ice myself; it was perfectly fresh, being simply the pure snow above converted into slush when it fell into the water.

The only hardship we suffered on these journeys was thirst, caused by the want of liquids in our diet. We breakfasted on cold boiled seal meat left over from our supper, dragged the heavy sleds from ten to fifteen miles, and re-erected the cumbersome tents at the conclusion of the march; then, when the day's work was ended, we sat down to our second meal, and received from the cooking-pot another ration of seal meat. No fruit, no vegetables; morning and night nothing but seal meat washed down with ice-cold water or hot broth. The pot of tea I made as soon as the tents were erected gave little relief to so many parched throats. One man drank two large cups of soup, two of tea, and nine of ice-cold water, all within the space of three hours. At times I myself almost rivalled his feat without either quenching my thirst or feeling that it was in any way abnormal.

Early in May we camped four miles from the south coast of Victoria Island, where the hunters could continue sealing, if they wished, or intercept the caribou as they grazed on the beach before proceeding inland. Sealing was the more profitable occupation, since the caribou were lean from long travelling and their meat satisfied the hunger of neither men nor dogs. Even their hides were useless, for the larvæ of warble-flies had profusely perforated them, and the long white fur of winter was beginning to shed and give place to a shorter coat of brown. But my companions, who had lived on seal meat alone for four months, craved variety, and the sight of caribou increased the desire. We divided our party; those who had only bows and arrows continued to watch over the seal-holes, and the three who possessed rifles hunted caribou, Ikpuck with a .44 Winchester, The Runner with a .22 Remington, and myself with a Ross Sporting .280.

Our first caribou hunt gave me some useful training for the days to follow. A man who had risen earlier than the rest sighted five caribou passing our camp a mile to the eastward, and awakened Ikpuck and me. We dressed hastily, and, without waiting for breakfast, raced at top speed for the shore to cut them off as soon as they landed. Breathless with the exertion, and perspiring in every pore, we took cover behind a low ridge eight hundred yards from the beach and waited for the herd to draw near. But the caribou loitered. Four weary hours we lay on the cold snow before they came within range, and then, through bad marksmanship, succeeded in shooting only one.

The Eskimos had many superstitions about the animals and birds; they taught me, for example, to throw away part of the liver of each caribou I killed, to propitiate its wandering spirit. Since the northward migration of the herds each spring, and their migration south again in the autumn, closely followed similar movements of the ptarmigan, the natives transferred to the bird some of the mysterious powers attributed to the caribou. So when Ikpuck shot a ptarmigan on his way back to camp he solemnly knelt in the snow and crooned a chant over its lifeless body. The chant was really a prayer, intended, like the throwing away of the caribou liver, to appease the spirits of the animals and ensure the success of our hunting.

Our little party, as now constituted, held more or less closely together during the next six months. My own immediate family, Ikpuck, Icehouse, and the two children, Jennie and Knife-Blade, have been introduced already; also The Runner, Icehouse's son, and his wife Leaf, who will figure largely in the coming pages. Icehouse's brother, The Listener, was a quiet old man who devoted much of his time to the care of his feeble wife. Their seventeen-year-old son Misty was Jennie's favourite companion; the two played at housekeeping together, snared small birds, and shot at ptarmigan with their bows and arrows. Chatterbox, a nephew of Icehouse, was a big, phlegmatic individual who abhorred quarrels and shirked the responsibility of ever taking the initiative. Himself a silent man, despite his name, his main trouble in life was to check the gossip of his wife, who outmatched Icehouse in her zeal for prying into the affairs of other people; but there was no malice in her gossip, and the two lived happily together, well liked by all their associates. Probably a physical peculiarity in Chatterbox contributed not a little to their matrimonial felicity; he was the only man in the country whose head was almost bald, and his wife was proud of his distinction. Why their seven-year-old son should be nearly as bald as his father was not easy to explain; it was certainly not due to disease, for these Eskimos had no infectious diseases.

Parted-Hair, the last hunter in our party, and the sole representative of Ikpuck's family line, was a young man who had married a woman twenty years his senior. His face was exceptionally short and flat, his nose almost swallowed up in his other features, so that even the most charitable of his countrymen could hardly call him prepossessing. Toward the children his manner was somewhat overbearing, but he always showed marked respect to his elders, especially to his kinsman Ikpuck. For the rest, he was an energetic hunter, a good sealer, and a very skilful fisherman, qualities that rank high in an Eskimo community. His marriage yielded him no children, but his wife, whose first husband had died a few years earlier, brought a fourteen-year-old son in her train.

Even the children had many little duties to perform in this our last camp on the sea-ice, while the fathers hunted seals and caribou, and the mothers sorted out the household things they intended to leave on the coast, or filled the pokes of blubber they were storing away for the autumn months. Each family had two pokes that weighed, when full, between three hundred and four hundred pounds, and our most pressing task for the moment was to dispose of them. Most people would have found it very unpleasant to cram a bag with oily seal blubber; but the women, accustomed to the task from childhood, merely put on their oldest clothes, rolled up the coat-sleeves, and buried their arms in the greasy mass without the slightest hesitation.

Not all the oil that exuded from the blubber found its way into the pokes. The women rubbed some of it over their faces to mitigate the effect of sunburn, and recommended the same treatment for my own weather-beaten countenance. Sunburn hardly seemed credible when the temperature of the atmosphere remained constantly below the freezing-point; but the sun now shone throughout the twenty-four hours of the day, and its light was doubled by reflection from the snow. So man, like the animals, changed his colour with the season. The faces of the Eskimos during the dark days of winter had been as fair as an Englishman's; now they were tanned to the deep rich brown of a southern European. One or two appeared to be darker still, but I strongly suspected that they could be appreciably lightened by a liberal application of soap and water.

Ikpuck and I conveyed his blubber pokes to a small island three miles off the coast, where we covered them with boulders to protect them from sea-gulls and foxes. The sea-gulls were easily deterred, but only a well-built cache could keep out the foxes, which worm their way into the smallest crevices. Before open water cut off communication with the shore, however, all animals would leave the island, and nothing could disturb our pokes throughout the summer.

Continual sealing began to pall on the Eskimos when the safe disposition of their blubber removed the last excuse for lingering on the sea-ice. The long winter had come to an end, and the midnight sun was shining over their heads. They forgot the monotonous hours of confinement within the dimly lighted huts, when the blizzards raged outdoors and the twilight of noon resembled night rather than day. The earth was awakening to life again after its long sleep. Ducks and loons flew overhead, the ptarmigan in the valleys were seeking out their mates, and a faint tinge of green had crept into the brown tips of the low dwarf willows that protruded above the snow. In the hills lay countless lakes teeming with trout and salmon, and herds of caribou grazed on the slopes and plains. Soon large pools would form around the margins of the lakes, and the unlocked waters race in foaming torrents to the sea. Everything beckoned us landward, to a joyous life in the open air. There would still be a few more snow-storms, succeeded by fogs and rain; later, dark clouds of mosquitoes would assail us night and day without rest. But there would be many days, too, of mild, clear weather when we could sleep beneath the open sky; and food was abundant everywhere, so that we could roam where we pleased, as free and unfettered as the caribou we hunted.

On May 9 our sleds climbed up the shore near the mouth of a large creek named Okowyarvik. The new life had begun.

# CHAPTER VII

## IN QUEST OF THE TORMIAT

VICTORIA ISLAND terminates to the west in a long and wide peninsula, to which early maps gave the name of Wollaston Land. Low hills averaging about 800 feet high form the backbone of the peninsula, and many large streams flow radially north and south out of the innumerable lakes that fill the valleys and depressions among the ridges. A thick layer of mud covers the greater portion of the land, but near the coast-line are cliffs of dolomite through which the streams have carved deep gorges. Not a tree rises anywhere. Mosses and lichens carpet the margins of the lakes, and here and there on the coastal plain grow patches of heather and dwarf willow; but the hills are brown and barren, or sparsely clothed with a few creeping plants such as dryads, saxifrages, and oxytropi.

On this peninsula I planned to live six months, isolated with my little band of Eskimos. The life on the ice was ended; fishing and caribou-hunting were to be our sole pursuits. As Ikpuck's adopted son I could observe all the details of Eskimo summer life, following its variations from day to day as no traveller had done before me. It was for this purpose, indeed, that I had cut myself adrift from the rest of the expedition until the winter, when the strait would freeze over again and allow me to return to Bernard Harbour. In the back of my mind lay also another plan. Sixty miles to the northward was Prince Albert Sound, the home of an Eskimo tribe that I had not yet visited. Each summer a few of the Sound people met and traded with Eskimos from Dolphin and Union Strait somewhere in the interior of Wollaston Land, and Ikpuck, who was born in this region, promised to guide our party to their usual places of rendezvous. He arranged that we should travel first to the Lake of Dancing within the Colville Hills; later, if necessary, to the Big Lake across the divide or to Prince Albert Sound itself.

We had landed near Okowyarvik Creek, which flows into a long, narrow harbour sheltered from every gale by an island that extends across its mouth. It was the

usual starting-point for Eskimos travelling to the
Great Sound, since the hills immediately north were
lower than at any other place either to east or west.
Okowyarvik means "the Home of the Dryad," not the
wood-nymph of that name, who could never find a
home in this desolate land, but the *Dryas integrifolia,*
a tiny flowering plant distantly related to our rose.
The Eskimos generally paid little attention to the
plants around them because they added nothing to
their food supply; but the dryad, heather, and willow
furnished their fuel during the summer months, and
in the hills heather and willow were not procurable.

We lingered a week at "Dryad Harbour," for the
season was still early and the snow that covered the
land would last another month. While the men were
hunting caribou the women overhauled their bags of
clothing, putting aside all the heavier garments not
needed again till winter. To these they added the
furniture of the snow-huts, the long wooden tables,
the drying frames, and a few of the stone lamps.
Each family made a separate pile of its possessions,
and on top of each pile the men deposited their sealing weapons, useless for the life on land. I myself
cached nearly all my provisions—pemmican, rice, oatmeal, hard bread, and tea sufficient to last me about a
month; only a little tea and cornmeal I retained on my
sled, to ease the transition from the "balanced" diet of

a European to the unvaried meat and fish of my companions.

Ikpuck and I deserted the main train on the march inland and wandered away in search of caribou. Small herds of three or four, mostly young bulls, showed up on every hand, but to approach them unseen was amazingly difficult. We circled for two hours around a herd that was grazing on the side of a low ridge, and just as we came within rifle range it suddenly moved its position, caught sight of us, and fled. We climbed the ridge cautiously, and saw three more caribou moving up the valley on the other side. I wished to fire at them when they came within three hundred yards, but Ikpuck, who thought they would approach still nearer, beckoned me to wait; instead of approaching they moved away, and disappeared from our view. A small hill lay ahead of us, which Ikpuck approached from one side, I from the other. As we drew near he discovered three caribou travelling in my direction, and, taking off his jacket, signalled to me to lie down; but I misread the signal, and in my haste to join him alarmed this herd also. Down in a valley a few miles farther on two caribou seemed to be moving toward a distant ridge. We gained its crest before them, built a low shelter of snow-blocks, and waited for them to draw near. One hour passed slowly by, then a second, and still they kept out of range. Chilled with the cold, we left our hiding-place and approached them from another direction. Ikpuck crawled near enough to shoot one of them in the leg; but his bullet inflicted only a flesh-wound, and the caribou with its mate galloped quickly out of sight.

Thus all day misfortune dogged our footsteps. We travelled perhaps thirty miles after our light break-fast at 7 A.M., and by nine o'clock in the evening I was almost exhausted. Then, as we wearily climbed the crest of a ridge, we came upon three fresh snow-blocks that our companions had placed in line to direct us to their new camp. Ikpuck passed them by with a brief glance; he refused to turn back empty-handed when caribou surrounded us on every side, and wished to continue the chase indefinitely, even though we slept on the uncovered snow. But I was less jealous of my reputation as a hunter, and with some difficulty per-suaded him to accompany me to camp.

Our companions had pitched their tents beside the first lake within the Colville Hills, a lake that abounded in two kinds of fish, lake trout and lake salmon, although it was only half a mile in diameter. Men, women, and children, scattered over its surface, were industriously chiselling holes through the thick ice or jigging their lines in the water below. The caribou meat in their camp had lost its attraction; they wanted to dine on fresh fish, which no one had tasted for six months. In less than two hours they hauled seven fine trout out of the lake, and but a short time afterward the children were scurrying from tent to tent with steaming messes of boiled fish.

I lay back among the caribou skins after supper, using my sleeping-bag for a cushion, and listened to Ikpuck's account of our day's adventures. A careless movement of my foot upset a tea-cup, emptying its contents onto one of our best robes. Icehouse sprang up indignantly. "You miserable wretch!" she exclaimed. "Do you think you are lying on sealskins? See what you have done. You have ruined our best robe." I cast an apologetic look at Ikpuck, who sat in the opposite corner. A faint smile flickered over his face, and his left eye gave a perceptible wink. Poor Ikpuck. Icehouse intercepted the wink, and, transferring her wrath, heatedly upbraided him for his indifference, while the old man silently hung his head. But her anger gave way to laughter as she helped me to scoop up the tea, and the incident became only a standing joke within our family circle.

We remained at the lake for several days, dividing our time between hunting and fishing. I was not familiar with their method of fishing and had better luck with the caribou. The Eskimos could stalk more skilfully, but my Ross rifle with its powerful coppernosed bullets was more effective than Ikpuck's .44 Winchester, The Runner's .22, and the bows and arrows that made up the rest of our armament. So they were always well pleased when I joined the hunting excursions.

Yet my "parents" were not satisfied. They wished me to become expert in fishing also. The caribou migration was almost ended; soon the herds would scatter far and wide, and fish alone be our mainstay until midsummer. Icehouse made a bag of sealskin to hold all the trout and salmon I would surely catch, and Ikpuck overhauled my fishing-line, fitting it with a barbless hook and bone sinker like his own. Then he wound it over a short stick notched at both ends, gathered up his own equipment, and invited me to my first lesson.

I have a vivid recollection of that lesson. We went out on the lake before noon, and with a chisel of native copper lashed to the end of a stout pole Ikpuck proceeded to dig a hole through the six-foot covering of ice. In twenty minutes he reached the water, making a hole fifteen inches in diameter at the top, four inches at the bottom. He then lowered his line until it touched bottom, rewound it about a foot, and began a rhythmical jigging.

"Take my chisel and make another hole for yourself," he said. Nothing seemed easier. I moved about twenty paces away and dug steadily for half an hour, but always there was more ice at the bottom of the hole. Ikpuck, who already had two trout on the ice beside him, looked over and laughed. "Come and

fish here," he called. "I will finish the hole for you."
We changed places, and I dropped my line into the
water. Presently I hooked a fish, which I hauled up
eagerly, hand over hand, as I had often done in boy-
hood; but it slipped off during a momentary pause in
the strain, for the hook was barbless. Afterward
Ikpuck taught me his own method of pulling in the
line, and the reason for the barbless hook. He used,
not his hands, but his wrists, rotating them alternately
against the cord so that the strain remained constant.
A barb was not only unnecessary, but a disadvantage,
because, in jigging, a fish is caught in the lip where
the flesh is tender, and a barbed hook often tears loose
where a barbless hook holds firm.

For an hour we had no more bites, so we crossed
some ridges and dug new holes in another lake, two
miles away. Here the light breeze of the morning suddenly increased to a violent gale. Ikpuck, considering
it part of the day's routine, sat on a snow-block with
his back to the driving snow and jigged his line as
patiently as in calm summer weather. I perforce did
likewise, though my feet seemed to grow colder and
more solid than the ice beneath. We returned to camp
at last with five trout and two salmon, one from my
hook, all the rest from Ikpuck's. But the lesson he
gave me bore fruit, for within a month I could dig
my own holes and catch as many fish as my companions.

Two short moves from this lake brought us to the

Lake of Dancing, where we hoped to meet the Tormiat
natives from the Great Sound. It was famous not on
account of its size—it was even smaller than the lake
we had just left—nor for its abundance of fish; but
because it lay near the watershed on the highway to
the Great Sound, and was encircled by many larger
lakes that provided good fishing until midsummer.
We set up our tents on one of several old camp-sites
around its margin, and settled down to await the
Tormiat.

During the next six days we scoured all the hills
around us, discovering a few caribou, but no natives
save two families that had separated from us on the ice
a month before. On every excursion we were joined
by Leaf, The Runner's wife, who had borrowed her
husband's .22 rifle to shoot at ptarmigan. I lent her
my own rifle on one occasion when we were stalking
a herd of caribou, and she killed a magnificent bull,
the finest we saw on Victoria Island. The other
women devoted all their time to fishing, and to drying
and caching the meat and fish that began to accumulate
in camp.

Spring was now advancing rapidly; so much snow
had melted from the hill-sides that sledding would soon
be impossible. At times the temperature rose above
40° F., though it dropped below the freezing-point
again at evening. Ptarmigan were mating in every
hollow, and the children launched many an arrow at

them with little success. On May 23 we saw the first
Lapland longspur, and three days later flesh-flies, the
forerunners of clouds of mosquitoes. In a pool of
water at the base of a hill lay a tiny mouse, drowned
by a sudden thaw before it could escape from its
burrow.

The increasing brownness of the hills made me
uneasy. We could discover no trace of the northern
natives, though some of them had visited the Lake
of Dancing the previous summer. Icehouse, who was
a medicine-woman, announced that she would enquire
at midnight from her guardian spirits, and our whole
party gathered inside the tent to hear the oracle. The
spirit of a wolf entered into her, and even thrust its
upper canines out of the corners of her mouth; but it
spoke in a mystic language that no one could interpret.
We thronged anxiously around it, beseeching it to
explain; and at last we heard this message:

"To Big Lake come your Great Sound kinsmen.
Travel thither with your sleds.
Before the snow flies turn ye back again."

The oracle was obeyed. By noon our little caravan
was slowly threading its way among the hills, heading
north-east toward Big Lake. Ikpuck guided the
course. The shoeing of frozen mud that once covered
the runners of his sled had fallen away at the Lake of
Dancing, and the bare wood grated harshly over the
snow. My own sled, following behind, glided along

easily on runners of steel. The Chatterbox and his family, who came next in the line, had abandoned their sled and hitched their dogs to a polar-bear skin that carried all their possessions. Last of all came Parted-Hair's sled, in the same condition as Ikpuck's. The Listener and his wife, too old to make unnecessary journeys, remained at the lake to watch over the meat and fish we had spread out on boulders to dry in the sun.

Twelve miles from the Lake of Dancing we sighted caribou and shot a large bull. We camped beside its carcass, and the women, who had failed to bring stone lamps and blubber, trusting to cook over open fires, searched the ridge-tops for fuel. But the season was less advanced on this side of the divide and vegetation scarcer, so that they found no fuel of any kind, not even the wretched dryad. I boiled a little venison for myself on the primus lamp, but the rest dined quite cheerfully on raw meat. Their tents, too, they had left behind, but they propped up two caribou robes for shelter from the breeze and spread out their sleeping-bags under the open sky. I fell asleep to the murmur of the dance-song they were practising for the meeting with the Tormiat from the Great Sound.

Big Lake, which we reached late the next evening, appeared to be circular in outline and about ten miles in diameter. We camped near its southern end, where we found old camp-sites, although the lake itself was silent and deserted. Icehouse summoned her guardian spirits again to confirm her former prophecy that the Tormiat were already on their way to visit us; and, with renewed hopes, we settled down to await their arrival, resuming our daily routine of fishing and the chase.

We waited in vain for four days, and even Icehouse became alarmed lest her prophecy should prove false. Believing that I might have mysterious powers beyond their comprehension she cunningly made me an accomplice in a third séance. She borrowed my two shirts of caribou fur, after I had turned into bed, bound them with her belt, and poised the bundle with the loose end of the cord. We expected her then to summon her guardian spirits and question them, discovering their answers by the weight of the shirts; but instead of summoning her own spirits she summoned mine, and bade me instruct them to lighten the bundle for "yes" and increase its weight for "no."

"The Tormiat will come tomorrow," my shirts announced.

"Is the bundle not lying?" asked The Runner, addressing himself to me.

The question embarrassed me; it seemed to reflect on my personal integrity. But how could I tell whether the Tormiat would come or not? I referred him back to Icehouse. "Ask Icehouse," I said. "She is a medicine-woman. She should know."

The Tormiat from the Great Sound did not arrive on the morrow. Instead, from their country came a blustering snow-storm that swirled and eddied around our camp for thirty-six hours. The wretched wind-breaks behind which the Eskimos crouched for shelter blew down in five minutes. My tent alone stood firm. It was 6¼ feet long, 5 feet wide, and 4 feet high, admirably adapted for one man, but a trifle small when Ikpuck and Icehouse shared it with me, as they did from now until autumn. Small or not, it was the only shelter that presented itself. While the men were building low walls of snow-blocks, and roofing them with sticks and skins into the semblance of dwellings, the women and children huddled inside my tent, one on top of another, and on top of Ikpuck and me, until the blizzard outside would have seemed a zephyr had we been able to reach it. But the door was blocked by a solid wall of humanity encased in fur, and the back of the tent was sewn to the floor-strips. Like bees in the centre of a hanging swarm, we almost suffocated; but we were warm.

The dogs howled all through the night, a big, grey-haired scoundrel being the worst offender. Icehouse, who had named it after her grandfather, yelled to it unceasingly, "Lie down there, my grandfather. You have done no work today. You have been well fed. Have you no bottom to your stomach?" The Eskimos in the neighbouring tents shouted every time they heard her voice. During brief lulls she complained to Ikpuck that the dogs were keeping his "son" awake. He merely rolled over in his bag and growled sleepily.

She sympathized with me the next day. "Grandfather was incorrigible last night, my adopted son. Did you hear him?" "Yes, Icehouse," I answered. "And I dreamed I heard your voice also. Were you talking?" The old lady laughed merrily. She dearly loved a joke, even at her own expense.

When the storm died away in the early morning Leaf left her shelter to seek some frozen caribou meat for breakfast. Far out on the lake she saw black specks in motion, and borrowed my binoculars to examine them. Her excited shout, "The Tormiat are coming, the Tormiat are coming," awakened the whole camp. We dressed in haste. Jennie, my little "sister," ran forward to meet them and assure them that we were friendly, while the rest of us lined up on the bank overlooking the lake to accord them a formal welcome.

The party drew nearer, and we distinguished two men and one woman, the latter carrying a small baby on her back. Cries of disappointment arose; instead of the thirty or forty visitors we had been expecting, here was only one family. True, a second family arrived a few hours later, but all the other Tormiat had gone far to the north-east, whither it was now impossible to follow them by sled. The wave of disappointment passed quickly, and every one was cheerful again before the strangers reached our camp. We helped them to set up their tent, nibbled some of their frozen seal meat, and hurried away to build a dance-house while the women stayed behind to gossip.

Our dance-house was not the orthodox dome of snow that I had seen in many settlements during the winter, for the roof would have melted and collapsed within twenty-four hours. Instead, we built a circle of snow-blocks three tiers high, and covered it with everything we could lay our hands upon. The rafters were fish-spears and walking-sticks, the roofing the canvas cover of my sled. As the canvas covered no more than half the roof my comrades requisitioned their tent skins to close the gap. They were now without tents again, exposed to any further gales that might arise; so they bundled all their possessions into the dance-house, piled them against the wall each morning, and sorted them out again in the evening at the conclusion of the dancing.

For three days we held high revel. All the formal dancing took place on the first day. My people were the hosts, and Icehouse, as the wife of the leading man, had the privilege of opening the ceremony. She performed her dance with much dexterity and grace, far surpassing the leading Tormiat woman, whose angular figure and awkward movements made me think of the puppets in a Punch and Judy show. The other Eskimos followed in the order prescribed by their age and party until the official program came to an end. Some of the more elderly natives, wearied with the eight hours' continuous performance, then retired to rest; but the younger kept up the dancing until early morning.

During the two days that followed, gossip and barter divided the hours with informal dances. Our visitors watched me furtively. Only one white man had crossed their lives before, and even he had vanished before they knew him intimately, or could assure themselves that he really came from that far-distant corner of the earth where a great pole props up the sky. They remembered the legend which said that Eskimos, Indians, and white men were originally brothers, their mother a beautiful woman who rejected every suitor until her father's dog, metamorphosed into a handsome young man, visited her and won her love. She herself went down to the ocean floor to preside over the waves, the fish, and the sea mammals; but her children scattered in all directions. Only the Eskimos remained human; the Indians kept their human forms, but became like wild beasts at heart; and the white men degenerated into monsters even in outward appearance.

So the Tormiat followed all my movements with the utmost curiosity. They still thought their legend partly true, and waited expectantly for evidence of my "monstrosity." Icehouse herself, my adopted mother, had scarcely outgrown the same beliefs. She asked more than one strange question about my people. "Was it true that some white men have arms that trail almost to the ground? Did my real mother have hair on her head like Eskimo women?" Not until I had lived with her family for six months, never leaving them for a single day, did she announce as a magnificent discovery, "You white men are just like ourselves." Even then she committed herself to no opinion concerning the "humanity" of white women!

The two tribes, having left most of their property at the coast, had little to exchange except songs. A quartet practised inside my tent each evening, Ikpuck and Icehouse teaching the new songs from Dolphin and Union Strait and learning the latest compositions of the Tormiat. Every one was happy until Ikpuck's handsome face struck a responsive chord in the heart of the leading Tormiat woman. She dared not reveal her inclinations while her husband sat by her side, but on the third evening, when he was unexpectedly called from the tent, she leaned forward, ignoring Icehouse and myself, pressed her nose to Ikpuck's and, drawing back, coyly awaited his response. But Ikpuck sat like a graven image, making no sign; and Icehouse veiled her anger under a wan smile. There was silence for an interval. Then footsteps crunched in the snow outside, and the woman, pushing aside the door of the tent, disappeared hastily.

Ikpuck turned to me. "Did you see her?" he asked. But Icehouse cut short my reply. "The ridiculous creature. She can't dance, she can't even sing, but she's shameless enough to make love to a handsome man like you, Ikpuck. Did you ever see such an uncouth woman?"

Her tirade seemed never-ending. Even Ikpuck wearied of it, though her flattering remarks about his good looks pleased his vanity. The poor woman was passionately fond of her husband, and the incident rankled in her memory for months. Gossiping with others she might mock the high-pitched voice and awkward gestures of her Tormiat rival, but in secret she brooded fearfully. She remembered her earlier widowhood, when her beauty was at its height and Ikpuck had divorced his first wife in order to marry her. They had hoped she would give him a son to sustain him in his old age; but their marriage was fruitless. Now she was growing old. Would he send her also away and take some younger woman who might grant him his heart's desire?

Icehouse had no reason for alarm. Ikpuck reciprocated her affection, and his thoughts never strayed to other fields. The old couple bickered like children, but their petty quarrels only held them more closely together. Every one knew that Icehouse's shrewd tongue concealed a generous heart, and little Knife-Blade, their adopted child, satisfied

Ikpuck's longing for a son. So their home life was complete.

Nevertheless the Tormiat woman disturbed Icehouse's peace of mind. She shrank from remaining in the same camp with her rival, and entreated Ikpuck to lead back our party to the Lake of Dancing. Ikpuck consulted me, and we agreed to depart on the morrow. The natives from the Great Sound joined us in a dance of farewell, and we started on the homeward march.

The snow was melting everywhere, and the women, skirting the ridges, filled their bags with dryads to cook our evening meal. We wandered along like bees, sipping at every thimbleful of water that collected in the cracked soil. A few pink saxifrages were opening out their blossoms, and Lapland longspurs sang gaily all around. My companions laughed and chattered as, marching steadily, we re-entered the Colville Hills. But when we approached a knoll slightly higher than the others Ikpuck raised his voice and wept shrilly. Yonder, on its crest, lay the bleaching bones of his only brother who had died six years before; and of all his family he alone remained. The whole train wailed aloud in sympathy, the hills echoed their cries, and the frightened longspurs crouched silent in the moss. Slowly our gloomy procession trailed past the fatal site; but when it lay far behind us my companions ceased their wailing and filled the air again with cheerful laughter.

Angmaloktok, the "Ever-Frozen," is one of the largest lakes within the Colville Hills. Its minimum diameter is about four miles, and the ice that covers its surface seldom vanishes even in the warmest summers. We entered a bay at its northern end, and while the Eskimos lingered to fish, I climbed a neighbouring hill to examine the country-side. North, south, east, and west, as far as the eye could see, stretched a wilderness of frozen lakes and barren ridges. No tree, no mountain, nothing to arrest the gaze except the black, ant-like forms of men and dogs moving about in the bay below. The sun, floating in a cloudless sky, cast no shadow to relieve the desolate monotony. So depressing was the landscape that I descended the hill and, without waiting to fish, started the train in motion again.

Ikpuck, as usual, headed the procession across the lake, and I followed him closely with my sled. One of my dogs, lamed in a recent fight, ran free, but Parted-Hair, who was travelling behind me, hitched it to the sled on which his wife and step-son were riding. I halted until he came up to me, quietly released the dog, and continued on my way. Parted-Hair was annoyed. He thought he could safely defy me among his people, and seized the dog again; and again I set it free without a remark. Another mile we traversed in silence; then, for the third time, he hitched the dog to his sled and refused to let it go, even though Ikpuck himself shouted a remonstrance. Parted-Hair was the stronger physically, but I held the winning card in this land where might is the only arbiter; he carried only a bow and arrows, while I had a rifle on my sled. I slung it over my shoulder, told Ikpuck to hold to his course, and waited for Parted-Hair and his sled. My action, of course, was sheer bluff; if nothing happened before he came up I intended no more than to cut the traces of all his dog-team. But to the natives, accustomed to the blood-feud, it meant certain death to my adversary, and they shouted a simultaneous warning. Parted-Hair liberated the dog in an instant, slunk to the back of his sled, and kept well in the rear of the caravan during the remainder of the march.

After we reached the Lake of Dancing that evening my companions held an indignation meeting outside my tent, and severely rebuked Parted-Hair for his arrogant behaviour. Presently his wife, pushing open the door, offered me a large trout; but I declined the peace-offering in order to magnify the gravity of his offence. She returned the next day with another trout, which I accepted, sending her away with the shoulder of a caribou I had just killed. This closed the incident. But Parted-Hair's attitude toward me changed; he became more respectful in his manner, and amply atoned for his previous conduct by many gratuitous services.

Ikpuck sat on a snow-block with his back to the driving snow.

Photo by K. G. Chipman.

It was a picturesque sight, this train of people and dogs stumbling over hill and lake.

*Photo by J. J. O'Neill.*

The caribou, or reindeer, is the camel of the Arctic.

*Photo by G. H. Wilkins.*

The men amused themselves at archery.

Dance-songs were their chronicles of current events.

Hungry children gathered round our tent.　　She carried it everywhere on her back.

Every morning at daybreak the hunters departed for the sealing-grounds.

Whenever a shoal gathered in the upper chamber they blocked its entrance and stabbed the struggling fish with three-pointed spears.

Weighted down with heavy packs, stumbling over a trackless land to a new fishing-lake in the hope of breaking their fast before another sleep.

# CHAPTER VIII

## BREAD FROM THE WATERS

OUR meeting with the Tormiat from the Great Sound fulfilled one of the purposes for which I had shaken off civilization and adopted the Eskimo life. It is true that we encountered but two families, and those for four days only; but in customs and language they so closely resembled the natives with whom I was travelling that it was unnecessary to visit the remainder of the tribe. My companions had welcomed the journey as a pleasant break in the routine of their daily life. Now that it was ended they resumed their regular duty at this season, the drying and storing away of fish for the barren months of early winter.

The long Arctic spring was drawing to its close.

Some of the smaller ponds had lost their covering of ice, and narrow lanes of water separated the still frozen lakes from their shore-lines. Ducks and loons, returning to their breeding-grounds, sought out old nesting-places in the mossy tundra or on grassy islets in the lagoons. The plumage of the ptarmigan was changing; their breasts preserved a wintry whiteness, but their backs became a faded brown hardly distinguishable from the vegetation around them. The females changed more rapidly than the males, as though nature had designed for them special protection; when they settled on snow their brown backs resembled the moss-covered boulders protruding above the surface, and in the meadows the white of their breasts shone like patches of unmelted snow. Life in many forms surrounded us, but caribou were lacking, for the countless herds that had migrated to Victoria Island from the south were swallowed up in the land. A month before, we had sighted five and six herds daily; now we saw fresh tracks, but rarely a single animal. The cows had dropped their calves in lonely valleys, and were lingering near them until they were strong enough to join the herds; and the bulls were wandering singly, or in twos and threes, here today and gone tomorrow, searching for the richest pastures.

From our camp on the Lake of Dancing we visited all the lakes within a radius of six miles. Our party split up each morning and drifted in different directions, each person carrying a fishing outfit, and the men their hunting weapons. Nine or ten hours later the women straggled back with their fish, bearing also, in fine weather, loads of dryads to cook the evening meal. They cut off the heads of the fish for the cooking-pots, threw the backbones and fins to the dogs, and spread the bodies on boulders, or across horizontal poles to dry in the sun. The whole party then reassembled an hour or two before midnight, and, squatting outside the tents, gnawed the fish-heads, bone by bone, and discussed the day's adventures. The hungry dogs looked on with mournful eyes; tied to stones, they dined miserably on bones and broth.

I hunted, most of this period, to obtain caribou meat for my starving dog-team, but during a fortnight's steady tramping saw but two young bulls, which we consumed entirely in three days. The stony ridges cut to pieces my light sealskin boots, intended only for soft snow, and Icehouse, who had tried to patch them each evening, finally rebelled. "Stop hunting for a time," she said. "Your boots are wrecked beyond repair, and caribou will be scarce until the warmer weather comes and the mosquitoes drive them near our camps. Stop hunting, and I will make you new boots with stouter soles for the summer months."

It was not only my boots that troubled her. She believed that an evil demon, haunting the hills to the westward where I generally made my excursions, trapped and destroyed the solitary hunter. In this very district, many years before, it had spirited away her first husband, who had vanished without leaving a trace. So when I, too, vanished for sixteen hours one day she became greatly alarmed, and entreated Ikpuck to lead a searching party. Willy-nilly, I had to join the fishermen and let my dogs go hungry.

The fish soon commenced to bite less freely in the surrounding lakes, and some of the men wandered farther afield. Ikpuck then shot a caribou eight miles away near the shore of Lake Ever-Frozen. Instead of packing it home, he buried it in the snow and advised moving our camp to its vicinity. Every one welcomed his suggestion and prepared back-packs for the dogs, since the melting of the snow on the ridges rendered our sleds useless until autumn came round again. We concealed in stone cairns the dried fish we had accumulated, raised the empty sleds on stone pillars, and piled on top of them all the stone lamps and other articles too heavy or too bulky to carry around with us during the summer; then, packing on our backs the remainder of the equipment, we abandoned the Lake of Dancing and marched away to our new home.

It was a picturesque sight, this train of people and dogs staggering over hill and lake under burdens almost equal in size and weight to themselves. The men carried the tents and weapons, the women the sleeping-gear, spare clothing, and cooking utensils, and the little children their own bedding and whatever else their strength permitted. With the packs lying horizontally across their backs they resembled from a distance dark crosses that crept over the snow, now strung out in irregular formation, now filing one behind another in single line, now clustering together with little movement as the train halted to rest. The dogs trailed behind the women and children, their packs, shaped like saddle-bags, beating against their ribs or grooving continuous furrows in the snow; but they, too, inherited the pioneering blood and adventurous spirit of their masters, and, in spite of their heavy burdens, curled their tails jauntily over their backs and cocked their ears at the alert.

Slowly we filed across Lake Ever-Frozen and deposited our loads on the shore of a deep inlet at its northern end. In a broad pool created by a stream that foamed down the hill-side a red-throated loon gaily dived and rose to the surface again. Ikpuck seized his fish-trident and raced over the ice to spear it; but just as he reached the margin of the pool the ice gave way, and plunged him in water to his waist. The loon flew up, and the mortified hunter returned to the bank to change his clothing. He had stripped off everything but his jacket—like a swallow-tail coat, it reached to his waist in front and hung down in a long tail behind—when a second loon settled in the same place. Despite Icehouse's loud remonstrances, despite the laughter of the rest of us, he raced for the pool again, the long tail alternately flapping between his naked legs and streaming in the air behind him. And again the ice gave way beneath him! Chilled to the bone, and thoroughly crestfallen, he hastened to the shore, and in a surly voice bade Icehouse unfasten the packs and set up the tent.

Our jigging in this corner of Lake Ever-Frozen was very productive for a week, and the new camp with its lines of drying fish among the dogs and tents soon became a replica of the one we had just abandoned. To stand on the ice hour after hour and mechanically vibrate a long line in the clear water below was a pleasantly monotonous occupation when the air was mild and the sunlight sparkled in the crystalline snow. Even when fogs rolled down on us, and only the dark water-holes at our feet relieved the whiteness all around, there was a comfortable peace in the atmosphere and in the mellowed voices that penetrated from somewhere unseen. The life was in fact too tranquil, too monotonous, for The Runner and his wife. They craved more activity, and spoke of hunting for caribou to the northward; and when they broached their project to me I rashly promised to accompany them.

We set out on a clear, bright morning and travelled from one ridge to another, pausing on each crest to search the surrounding country. No caribou were visible, but two hares started up beneath our feet and fled to the extreme edge of the snow-patch. They seemed to know that their coats had not yet changed to a summer brown, for they crouched there, half invisible, until we almost walked on top of them; then, flashing white on the dull clay, they sped across to the next snow-patch and again crouched motionless. But a hunter who lives by the chase feels no pity for his victims, and both animals, despite their pathetic ruses, soon dangled over The Runner's shoulder.

The sky clouded in the afternoon, and a fierce snowstorm broke in our faces, blotting everything from view. It was useless to keep on travelling, for a caribou might pass unseen within ten yards of us; it was equally useless to turn back and wander for hours vainly seeking the camp. We looked around for shelter. There was none; no cliff, not even a boulder. The Runner and I sat on the snow, shoulder to shoulder, backs to the wind; while Leaf, his wife, crouched in the angle between our outstretched legs. After a long half-hour the storm began to pass over. When I mentioned the change to my companions Leaf raised her head and smiled. The Runner did not hear; with folded arms and head drooping on his chest he was sleeping.

We circled back toward the tents after the gale abated, and in spite of the light fog that still hung over the landscape stumbled on two young bulls, both of which we shot. The heads and limbs we buried in the snow to collect the following day; The Runner took one of the carcasses on his back, I took the other, and Leaf carried the two hares. After we had proceeded thus for about a mile The Runner changed burdens with his wife, who accepted without a murmur. I promptly changed with him, and a few minutes after with Leaf again, giving her back the hares. But packing was still a new experience to me, and though I reached the camp without mishap, I deeply rued my gallantry the next morning when a thousand pains shot through my neck every time I turned my head.

A fortnight's fishing exhausted the bay and compelled us to make another move. It mattered little which way we turned, for every ridge bounded a lake that contained both trout and salmon. But since the total catch would be greater if we scattered our forces and settled on different lakes the families separated. The Listener went south, The Chatterbox north, Parted-Hair north-east, and Ikpuck and The Runner east.

This dispersal of the individual families completed one half of the strange cycle through which the Eskimos passed year after year. They reacted to the seasons, to their constantly changing environment, more than most of the inhabitants of our globe. The problem of obtaining life's basic needs, food, clothing, and shelter, left little time for other thoughts; and the seals and caribou that furnished them with food, furnished also the materials for clothing and tents. In winter, when the land lay bare and silent beneath the snow, when the caribou had migrated south, when the twilight hours were brief and the nights long, the natives had banded together into tribes, and tribe combined with tribe to wrest a precarious livelihood from the frozen sea by united effort. Food had been common to all, and their snow-houses had adjoined each other so closely that the families seemed absorbed in the group. With the returning sun and lengthening days nature had recalled its life; the seals had appeared on top of the ice, the caribou had come northward again, and the tribes of Eskimos had broken up into little bands. For a time they had lingered on the ice to hunt more seals; then, turning landward, they had pursued the caribou over the snow-covered hills and plains. Now the snow was vanishing, the caribou had scattered, and fish alone provided a sure livelihood until midsummer. So my party, like many another throughout the country, was dividing into its constituent households, each of which now toiled for itself alone. The tribe no longer existed; society had dissolved into its first element, the family.

The dissolution was not completed in one day. Although the other families scattered, those of Ikpuck and The Runner remained united for a short time longer, wandering eastward together to a district as yet unvisited, and therefore more likely to harbour caribou. After two days' marching we set up the tents on the shore of a small lake and discussed our hunting program. Ikpuck and The Runner agreed to scour the land to the northward, where the hills sloped away toward Big Lake. I myself chose the higher land to the south-east, whence I could gain a wider view of the country and perhaps discover some rock-exposure that would indicate the geological formation. Leaf wanted to go with her husband, and Jennie insisted on sharing their fun. As for Icehouse, she was content to fish near camp with little Knife-Blade.

We went our several ways in the morning, but an hour after we separated a dense fog settled over the land. I turned back immediately, and by good luck gained the camp again. Some of the dogs were prowling among the tents, and Icehouse and Knife-Blade were fishing just below, but of Ikpuck and his party there was no sign. I sent Knife-Blade home to guard the camp and fished in the lake all day with Icehouse. From time to time the fog lifted for a few minutes, but closed in again as densely as before. Toward midnight, when the light faded a little, we returned to the tents, ate some dried fish, and tumbled into our sleeping-bags.

Icehouse became alarmed when the fog continued unchanged next day. She knew that the hunters were in no danger of starvation, for they all carried fishing-lines. Even if they were unable to cook their fish they were no worse off than ourselves, for the few dryads growing round our camp were too damp even to smoulder, and the semi-dried fish we ate for breakfast and supper were hard on the outside, but perfectly raw within. It was the exposure she dreaded, especially for her little daughter Jennie. She fretted about the child all through the morning, and several times I heard her cry to the fog, "Go away. No one wants you. You make us cold and uncomfortable;" just as white children call to the rain:

> "Rain, rain, go to Spain,
> Never show your face again."

Her anxiety increased toward evening, and she adopted sterner measures. She tied a cord around her face to distort her features, and with a set fox-trap in one hand and a knife in the other, defied the fog with threats and mocking laughter. Knife-Blade and myself, holding her arms, echoed her mockery. "You're a pesky nuisance," she cried, flinging the trap to the ground, where it sprang with a snap. She thrust the two weapons into my hands, distorted my face, and bade me intimidate the fog in the same way; and I repeated her cries, adding a few words of honest English for good measure. Then she re-entered her tent, rolled my jacket into a bundle, and summoned into it, one by one, all the offended spirits that had occasioned the untimely weather. Some were the shades of white men; I named them for her, Jack, Bob, Mary, Jane, and soothed them with fair words until they departed. Others, that were the shades of Eskimos, she herself propitiated in like manner, and banished with her knife a few that seemed loth to depart. At last her efforts succeeded; the jacket told her that the atmosphere would clear on the morrow, and, greatly relieved, she retired to her sleeping-bag to await the result.

An east wind sprang up in the morning and the fog lifted. "Look," she cried, issuing from the tent. "Yesterday we assailed the fog and it has vanished." Ikpuck and his party appeared about noon, weary, but otherwise none the worse for their experience. Thinking it useless to search for the camp until the weather cleared they had wandered about, fishing in different lakes, and huddling together at night on patches of bare ground. Ikpuck had shot a bull caribou that strayed near them, and they had satisfied their hunger with the marrow and back fat, seasoning them with raw fish.

The Runner now decided to move to a lake farther north where they had caught many fish during their late excursion; but Ikpuck wanted to continue eastward in search of more caribou. The former departed first. We watched his family disappear over the ridge, then packed up our own equipment and marched away. So our last link with the tribe was severed, and the dispersal of the band complete.

A T-shaped lake larger than most of the lakes in the vicinity was the site of our next camp. We deposited our packs on its shore and went out on the ice to fish.

Ikpuck and I dug holes, but Icehouse wandered over to a sun-lit pool at one corner and dropped in her line. It hooked a trout even before it touched bottom, and in the space of four hours she drew from this one spot twenty-nine trout and two salmon, although Ikpuck and I, who dug holes not a hundred yards behind her, caught only ten trout between us. It may have been the sunlight alone that attracted the fish; more probably the stream that rushed down the neighbouring slope washed many insects into the pool and made it an unusually rich feeding-ground.

My family thoroughly enjoyed the solitude and freedom of our new camping-place, where we could come and go, eat and sleep, as fancy moved us. The children, Jennie and Knife-Blade, counted this period a holiday, and when fishing grew monotonous, stripped off their clothes and splashed in the water, or snared the longspurs and sandpipers, or shot at ptarmigan with their bows and arrows. Sometimes they vanished for several hours, and returned in the early morning, while we were sleeping, merely to eat and rest before their next excursion. Their parents imposed no restraints on them and exacted no duties. Whenever they were absent, and Icehouse wanted to cook, Ikpuck, forgetting the pride of a hunter, would fill

her bag with dryads and bring her water from the
lake. No eye but mine saw his undignified conduct,
and I was one of the family.

Leaving Icehouse here at her fishing, Ikpuck and I
went east to look for caribou. The succession of ridges
and lakes continued unbroken, and by dropping our
lines here and there through promising cracks in the
ice we captured five trout. In the evening we sighted
our first caribou, two bulls grazing in a meadow of
green moss beside a distant lake. There was no cover
within a thousand yards, but we stalked them patiently
for several hours and at last managed to crawl near
enough on hands and knees to drop both animals at
the first volley. Then, piling the carcasses in a heap
for Icehouse and Jennie to bring in later, we started
back for camp fifteen or more miles away, packing only
the skins and hind-quarters. I was very weary, for
we had travelled twenty-four hours and eaten nothing;
and once, as we rested on the brow of a hill, I fell
sound asleep. But Ikpuck gently wakened me, saying
that our limbs would grow stiff if we lingered too long;
and to beguile the march he related quaint stories of
the Eskimo "long ago." Most of them were about
birds and animals, and resembled Æsop's fables without the morals. Although I was too weary to pay
much heed to them, one story concerning a giant
remained in my memory.

"You remember Putulik," he said, "the island where

we built our snow-huts last winter; and that other island near it, Ahunga-hungak, which you passed so often with your sled. Long ago, at midsummer when the ice had melted or moved away, some of our people living on Putulik beheld a giant wading across the sea, a giant so tall that his knees stood out above the water and his head seemed to touch the sky. Our people hid in terror among the crags. He landed on Ahunga-hungak, and, seated on its summit, juggled with two rocks that ten men like you and I could hardly move; each time one dropped into his hand a report like a gunshot reached the Eskimos' ears. But our medicine-men, who were more powerful then than they are today, chanted a spell against him. He rose to flee, and in two strides reached the water's edge; but there he fell, and his body changed to a crag. The winds and waves have washed most of it away, but in my childhood we could still see the red belt that encircled his waist. Now that also has disappeared, and only his nose and eyebrows remain. Next winter I will show you his juggling stones, lying on the island's top where he dropped them in his flight."

Soon after this hunting trip, Parted-Hair and his family appeared and pitched their tent beside us. Fortune had not been kind to them, for they had seen no caribou and caught only a moderate quantity of fish. Nevertheless, since they were the visitors, etiquette obliged them to open up their packs and present each of us with a morsel of dried trout. It may seem strange that such close kinsmen should insist on a formal display of hospitality and goodwill, but Eskimos, like all human beings, are slaves to customs of their own creation.

The increasing number of cracks in the ice, and of deep pools round the margins of the lakes, induced Ikpuck and Parted-Hair to adopt another mode of fishing. In place of the hook and sinker on their lines they attached the gleaming tooth of a polar bear, and whenever a fish approached this lure promptly transfixed it with a long-handled trident fitted with three bone barbs. They even waded out into the water and chased the fish back and forth until the survivors escaped under the ice. The latter method was so successful that they often speared in twenty minutes twice as many fish as the rest of us caught in a day; but it required amazing endurance, for their blood almost coagulated at times and their limbs became stiff and black. One could readily account for Ikpuck's rheumatism, though he himself would not have understood the explanation. I noticed that nearly half their catch consisted of salmon-trout, weighing, on an average, only three or four pounds, whereas the salmon-trout that migrate from the sea each year to spawn in lakes nearer to the coast average between eight and ten pounds. Evidently their growth is stunted by permanent imprisonment in fresh water. They become, too, more sluggish, for though the lake trout will take the hook at any season of the year, we caught no salmon-trout until the ice began to melt and lanes of open water encircled all the lakes.

Several red-throated loons and Pacific eiders nested in our vicinity. The loons always build on swampy islets or on tiny peninsulas nearly severed from the shore. Each female lays two eggs, but the nests are so close to the water-line that one and even both eggs often become chilled and fail to hatch. Of the young that do hatch some are devoured by hawks, others by lake trout, which are almost as voracious as the pike of more southern waters. Nevertheless the bird is common in every part of the Arctic, so that its longevity must compensate for the low fecundity and heavy death-rate. The eiders build on dry land either near the margins of the lakes or on the hill-sides immediately above; and in their nests we invariably found from four to seven eggs. If every egg hatched, and the offspring continued to breed at the same rate, the population would treble itself within ten years, even discounting the short span of life of the individual bird and the destruction of the young by hawks and lake trout. But other agencies operate to check its increase, not the least active being the white foxes, which prey the more heavily on eider eggs because they are easily discovered and readily accessible. Thus by lowering the fecundity of the loons, and increasing the mortality of the eiders, nature keeps the numbers in both species within definite limits.

The bows and arrows of the Eskimos inflicted but little damage on these water-fowl. I once came upon Parted-Hair after he had vainly discharged all his arrows at a loon that was swimming in the corner of a lake. Using an ice-cake for a raft, and his fish-spear as a pole, he was gathering up the feathered shafts, one by one, as they danced upright in the water, while his step-son and Jennie tried to prevent the bird's flight by racing along the ice-edge and shouting whenever it raised its head above the surface. The chances were all in favour of the loon when I ended the chase with a bullet.

The days grew warmer and more pleasant as spring gave place to summer. Yet its coming was not an unmixed blessing, for it hatched out myriads of mosquitoes that rose and fell in the atmosphere like the motes in a sunbeam. How so many could exist was a mystery. Wherever we travelled they hovered around us like bees swarming, and no smudge could keep them at bay. My tent became the common refuge, for its doorway of fine netting resisted all their assaults, though they pattered on the roof like rain. Outside every one wore mittens as in winter, and my companions beat their faces with loon skins as automatically as a band-conductor wields his baton. Only on the ice could we escape the insects, their flight being limited to about a quarter of a mile, unless the wind carried them farther. The animals suffered almost as much as ourselves. Our dogs tried to burrow in the ground to protect their feet and noses, and a young bull caribou, blinded by the cloud of mosquitoes that swarmed around its head, trotted within fifty yards of me without noticing my presence.

The warm weather, too, enlarged the lanes of water round the margins of the lakes and increased the difficulty of crossing onto the ice. Ikpuck therefore decided to return to Lake Ever-Frozen, which, from its size, remained ice-bound all or most of the summer. We first packed the dried fish one stage ahead, then returned for the camping-gear, and, thus travelling, reached in four days the eastern end of the lake not far from our old camping-place. The other families in the band had gathered there already, reunited by the same problem of food supply that a few weeks earlier had caused their dispersal.

My two months of practical training should have rendered me a past master in the fishing technique of my companions, but at this lake they taught me a new device. The largest trout always lay deepest, but none of our lines would reach the bottom of the lake. Moreover a long line, if drawn up quickly hand over hand—or wrist over wrist, in true Eskimo fashion—invariably tangles. Ikpuck's method was to lower his line to the last inch, and, when a fish struck, to run backward from the hole, slowing down to a walk as the end of the line approached the under surface of the ice. The fish, half drowned by its rapid ascent, had then no time to jerk itself free of the hook, although it might easily tear loose if it struck the edge of the fishing-hole. By slowing down to a walk, Ikpuck could govern its passage through the ice with more caution.

For the guidance of the uninitiated angler I should add two rules that the Eskimos have tested and found useful. Respect the craving of trout and salmon for water by turning the heads of your catch toward the pool; then others will surely gather to your hook and seek to join their brethren on the ice. Secondly, when you lower your line into the water again, do not forget to say, "Encore, encore, give me another."

The rules concerning diet I cannot recommend with the same confidence. The Eskimos, who knew no vegetables save the semi-digested moss in the stomachs of the caribou, ate only meat and fish, preferably boiled, for second choice dried or frozen, and raw when necessary. Here in the Colville Hills scarcity of fuel made boiled fish a luxury that we could enjoy only two or three times a week. Breakfast consisted always of a half-raw fish taken from a drying-pole and consumed usually in one's sleeping-bag; dinner did not exist, and supper was boiled fish on lucky days and the same as breakfast on unlucky. The digestions of my companions seemed proof against every outrage, but my own rebelled. An insidious dysentery attacked me, making me at last so weak that I could hardly drag myself to the fishing-ground. My throat became dry like parchment, and drinking the clear water in the fishing-holes merely aggravated the dysentery without relieving the thirst. Altogether my predicament was rather alarming.

No parents could have been kinder to me at this time than were Ikpuck and Icehouse. Believing that all disease had a supernatural origin, Icehouse tried to exorcise the agencies responsible for my ill-health. That she failed to cure me distressed but did not surprise her, for, as she herself remarked, Eskimo remedies had no efficacy with white men. She showed her sympathy in a more practical manner by giving me the choicest morsels of fish, and by foraging far and wide for dryads in order to cook more frequently. Yet in spite of all her efforts my health failed to improve, and at last I sent The Runner to the Lake of Dancing to bring me a few ounces of malted milk and three pounds of dog-pemmican that I had stored there in a cache. The malted milk lasted me two days, after which I began on the pemmican, prepared forty years earlier for the fur posts of the Hudson's Bay Trading Company. It was brown with antiquity, and consisted merely of dried beef crushed to powder, with here and there fragments of bones; but mixed into a paste with cold water it was more digestible than the half-raw fish on the drying-poles, and more palatable than saltless fish boiled over a smoky flame in a cupful of water. So for a week I ate nothing but pemmican. Gradually the dysentery lessened, my strength began to return, and, though the intolerable thirst continued, there was hope of a permanent recovery if in some way we could improve our diet.

I talked the matter over with Ikpuck. He could understand my dislike of raw fish, but not its effect on my health, unless, indeed, my guardian spirit had forbidden its consumption. Yet he would gladly do anything to aid my recovery. It was the end of July; the fur of the caribou was in its prime, and the fishing season nearing its close. He had intended to pass the remainder of the summer wandering in the hills to the north-east, where caribou were numerous but fuel scarce; however, seeing that I might eat nothing but cooked food, we could move southward toward the coast if I wished, and travel over plains amply clothed with heather and willow. We agreed to adopt this second plan and communicated the decision to our companions.

A snow-storm, not an unusual occurrence even in the height of summer, delayed our departure a few days; but as soon as the snow melted again we packed all our fish to the Lake of Dancing and cached it with our other possessions. Then we turned southward, away from the hills and their fishing-lakes to the plains nearer the coast. Once more a change in the season had altered the course of our wanderings and directed our energies into a new channel.

## CHAPTER IX

### ON THE TRAIL OF THE CARIBOU

THE caribou or reindeer, for the two are identical, is the camel of the Arctic, the animal that transforms a barren waste into a hospitable dwelling-place for man. Domesticated, it transports his possessions and supplies him with milk; and tame or wild, it furnishes most of his needs. My Eskimos had no knowledge of its domestication, but they made clothing and tents from its fur, straps and lines from the tanned hide, tools and weapons from the bones and antlers, ornaments from the teeth and toes, and thread and cord from the sinew of its back and legs. Every part of the animal thus had its use; but much was often wasted, especially at the end of summer, when the natives had wandered far from their sleds and

winter sealing-grounds. They needed its fur for clothing, seven whole skins making only a single costume
that lasted at the most three years; so they slaughtered
bulls, cows, and calves, took the hides, the sinew, the
back fat, and what little meat they could carry, and
abandoned the rest to the wolves and foxes. Such
indiscriminate destruction might have been branded as
foolish, even criminal; but when white men have unconsciously exterminated the buffalo by similar methods,
how can we expect a primitive people like the Eskimos
to make regulations for the preservation of their
game? After all, no regulations were necessary as
long as their only weapons were bows and arrows,
which exacted too light a toll to cause any diminution
in the herds of caribou that returned to their Arctic
grazing-grounds year after year. Only if conditions
changed, if the natives became armed with the deadly
magazine rifles of our modern civilization, would there
be any reason for limiting the number a hunter might
kill, or prohibiting the slaughter of females and young.

As we wandered southward, every eye in the party
was strained for the sight of caribou. We secured our
first trophy where the hills merged gently into the
plain, and gave our dogs the feast for which they had
hungered many weeks. From here on, patches of
dwarf willow and heather, the fuel we had lacked so
sorely in the hills, alternated with meadows of lichens
and moss, or with wide stretches of stony ground

almost devoid of vegetation. We stumbled over a bed of dolomite split by frost into rectangular blocks, its resemblance to the floor of an ancient temple heightened by two stone pillars erected several years before to support a kayak or hunting canoe. A mile or two beyond a caribou caught our scent, whisked up its tail, and bounded out of sight behind a low ridge. We could see a fair-sized stream in the distance tumbling among the rocks; and there Ikpuck instructed us to camp while he pursued the caribou that had just disappeared. Twelve hours later, when every one was asleep, he returned, and, pushing open the door of my tent, displayed the skins of two caribou; their carcasses he had left side by side for the women to bring in, merely aligning some boulders on top of a knoll to guide them in their search. Icehouse and Jennie dressed and departed immediately with dogs and packlines. The howling of the other dogs aroused the camp, and a second party went out to look for more caribou. So, for one reason and another, we lingered in this spot nearly three days.

Instead of hunting during this interval, I made a collection of all the plants growing around us, and enjoyed two swims in a neighbouring pool. A bath is a rare luxury in the Arctic, where there is often no water to wash even the face and hands. My companions solved the problem by never washing. Contact with the snow in winter purified them, and in summer the deep tanning of their skin masked its uncleanliness. It was easy to discover one reason for the peculiar atmosphere of an Eskimo throng. The odour was really a composite one, the smell of fur clothing mingling with the distinctively human odour that characterizes all races, but differs in each one. Neither Eskimo society nor our own ever discusses this topic, although Icehouse once confessed to me in private that her people had found the odour of the white man very disagreeable. However that may be, my bathing, being purely voluntary, certainly excited much interest, and when I stole away to the pool for the second bath, Ikpuck notified the whole party. Innocently devoid of clothes, I was disporting gaily in the water when the sound of voices made me look up. Men, women, and children lined the bank above me, intently watching the exhibition. None of them knew how to swim, or even that it was possible, and they gasped with admiration when I dived out of sight and reappeared a few yards away. *Honi soit qui mal y pense.* Ikpuck, The Runner, and even the latter's wife stripped off their clothes immediately and joined me in the water, eager to receive a first lesson in the newly discovered art.

We were now so close to our caches on the coast that my companions decided to deposit there, before turning westward, the small quantity of dried fish they were carrying against emergencies. The visit enabled

me to take from my own cache a little rice and pemmican, which, being more easily digested than boiled
meat, would assist my return to health. The pemmican
I carried on my back, but most of the rice I placed in
the pack of my largest dog, who ruined it a few hours
later by plunging headlong into a deep pool. During
the two days immediately following we secured no
game of any kind, so that I was driven to share the
pemmican with my companions. Hungry as they were,
I could hardly induce them to touch it, although they
would have killed without compunction any fellow-
countryman who attempted to hoard food when they
were starving. I was different, they averred, and their
ways were not my ways; deprived of my special food,
I might be prostrated again by a return of my illness.
Their children might eat a little, if I so desired, but
as for themselves, they were accustomed to hunger,
and would surely kill a caribou on the morrow, or, if
not then, on the day following. In the end, however,
they agreed to compromise, and divided up half my
pemmican, leaving the other half for myself.

Our usual procedure at this time was to march from
ten to fifteen miles, then to scatter out in search of
game while the women pitched camp. Ikpuck, The
Runner, and myself, going out together late one afternoon, discovered a large bull caribou grazing in the
centre of an open plain where it would certainly detect
us if we attempted to approach. In spite of this The

Runner, after a short consultation with Ikpuck, walked boldly forward, stooping slightly, and holding over one shoulder a walking-stick, over the other his .22 automatic. Ikpuck, stooping similarly, fell in line behind him, I behind Ikpuck, and we zigzagged slowly over the plain, drawing nearer and nearer to our quarry. Once it raised its head and watched us so closely for a full minute that I expected it to bound away in alarm; but, evidently reassured by our appearance and rambling movements, it resumed its grazing and paid no further attention to us. So we were not more than three hundred yards away when, at a signal from The Runner, I sank on one knee and dropped the animal with a bullet behind the shoulder.

Why did the caribou not flee? Doubtless because it mistook us for another caribou idly approaching from a desire for companionship. The fur of our clothing was the same as its fur, and from a distance the stick and rifle above The Runner's head might fairly pass for antlers. Moreover, caribou trust more to scent than to vision, and we were careful to keep on the lee side. This bull was really less sociable, or less curious, than the majority; two or three weeks later, when Ikpuck and The Runner were stalking another bull, the former concealed himself with his rifle behind a low mound and The Runner, impersonating a caribou grazing, lured the animal within easy range without even advancing.

During one of our hunting excursions, Ikpuck initiated me into a method of cooking meat different from the usual process of boiling. We had shot a caribou ten miles in advance of our party, close to a tilted bed of dolomite that broke away in large, thin slabs like roofing slate. With four of these slabs he built a Dutch oven against a low bank, strewed the top slab with moss and moistened it with water from a neighbouring pool; he then laid his slices of meat and back fat on the moss, covered them with an inverted sod of fresh, green grass, and lit a fire inside the oven. As the under-side of the meat broiled he turned it over and remoistened it. When cooked it was both tender and appetizing, though the moss gave it a rather peculiar flavour. To relieve our hunger while the steaks were broiling he also roasted in the fire two leg-bones and the liver. The bones cooked in about three minutes, and, when the ends were broken, the marrow flowed out like melted butter. Huxley says that only savages eat marrow; if that be true, our epicures are neglecting one of nature's choicest viands. It may be, however, that taste varies with environment, for when Anderson mailed some dried back fat to my office a few years later I nibbled one small piece for old times' sake and threw the remainder out of the window.

As we travelled on we came to a deep gorge where a large stream cut through the final line of hills, barring its passage to the sea. To the north lay a broad, sandy plain, the bed of an ancient lake, and beyond, an isolated, rounded hill flanked by soft meadows that were certain to harbour caribou. We all forded the stream without mishap except Jennie, who had dropped behind when readjusting the packs of two dogs. I went back to look for her, while the others pushed on across the plain. The poor child was nearly a mile in the rear, still struggling cheerfully with the ill-balanced packs that persisted in slipping under the animals' bellies. I rearranged them for her, and we hurried on to overtake our companions; but a fierce sand-storm now swept the plain, and our progress was slow and painful, with frequent returnings to urge on the dogs. Dogs and storm combined delayed us so greatly that the hunters, tired of waiting for us at the hill, went on ahead to intercept a herd of caribou they had sighted, leaving little Knife-Blade to watch for me and request me to join them with all speed.

This hunt well illustrated the unity of an Eskimo band. Every individual, man, woman, and child, took part in it—except The Listener's wife, who, being old and feeble, remained to guard the packs; and both men and women contributed to the discussion that decided the tactics to be employed. At the foot of the hill stretched a lake three-quarters of a mile in diameter, and, beyond it, a wide, grassy plain where fifteen caribou were grazing. The plain rose in a gentle incline toward the west, where it dropped abruptly down to another lake. The Eskimos planned to make the fullest use of these topographical features by enclosing the caribou within a long rectangle of which the lake and ridge formed two adjacent sides. On the other long side, parallel with the lake, they built low mounds of turf twenty or thirty yards apart that from a distance resembled the black heads of half-concealed men; and here and there, where the ground was low, they set up their jackets on walking-sticks, or left a child to rise to his feet and frighten the caribou back. The fourth side, from the end of this "fence" to the eastern extremity of the lake, they left open until they should take up their positions behind the ridge, when the women, at a given signal, would close the gap and drive the caribou toward them.

When Jennie and I arrived at the camp the hunters had already given the signal and the women were preparing to carry out their part of the program. I accompanied them, as it was then too late to join the firing-line. The caribou scented us half a mile away and fled down the wind to the crest of the ridge; but there the bullets and arrows of the hunters rained among them, turning them back toward us. The women shouted and waved their arms, I opened fire with my rifle, and the terror-stricken animals stampeded back again; one swam the lake and passed our camp, two dashed through the "fence" of turf and children, and the remainder, fleeing to the ridge, drew back before another volley. Three times we drove them back and forth in this way before the survivors broke through our lines, leaving eight of their number dead or dying on the hunting-field.

My Ross rifle failed me twice during this action. Once I had trouble in closing the breech, and once the firing-pin struck so lightly that the cartridge failed to explode. In both cases the cause was probably the same, a little sand that had blown into the leather holster when crossing the storm-swept plain. I had carefully cleaned the weapon before using it, but evidently a few particles of sand still remained in the bolt. It was this same defect in the Ross rifle that created so much bitterness in the early months of the great European war, and finally led to the re-arming of the Canadian troops with the British Lee-Enfield.

My companions, elated by the success of their hunt, feasted and idled for two days. The reasons they offered were excellent; drizzling rain made travelling unpleasant, the meat we had accumulated was more than we could carry, and the green hides needed to be scraped and dried. But the principal reason remained subconscious. For a few hours, or for two or three days, they could display phenomenal energy— even the children were inured to sleepless hunting trips of thirty-six hours' duration; but they could not plod along, day after day and week after week, at an even rate of progress, because this sustained effort involved a mental strain to which they were totally unaccustomed. We had travelled long and far for three days, and they needed an interval to recuperate. During those three days, too, they had suffered from hunger, for we had killed no game; and now they gorged themselves so freely that involuntarily I thought of Icehouse's reproach to the dogs, "They have no bottoms to their stomachs." The human body is remarkably plastic; through generation after generation these Eskimos had developed something of the nature of the camel, being capable of taking in a few hours sufficient nourishment to compensate for one period of scarcity and to carry them over another.

During these days of idleness they indulged in various pastimes. They set up a clod of turf about a foot square, and, standing back forty paces, shot at it with their bows. Only about one arrow in twenty hit the target, so that either their marksmanship was poor or their bows very inferior. Since they had all practised archery from childhood, and two of the men, Ikpuck and The Runner, were noted hunters, the fault evidently lay in their bows. These belonged to the type technically known as "composite," like the well-known Tartar bows. The framework was of three pieces of wood rudely jointed together, two end pieces or horns curving backward and a middle piece. All the back of the wood was covered with a narrow band of sealskin, over which was lashed a pair of stout cords of twisted sinew. It was the sinew that gave the weapon its spring, for the frame was merely drift-wood picked up on the beach, or spruce of the poorest quality. Such crude materials, added to crude work-manship, made the balance very uneven, so that although the maximum range of the weapon was about one hundred and twenty-five yards, its effective range hardly exceeded twenty-five. Indeed, I have seen The Listener miss a caribou that passed not more than fifteen yards away.

While the adults amused themselves at archery beside the camp the children played their own games on the slope above. They set up fences of turf to enclose fictitious caribou, and dug shallow pits from which to shoot their arrows; or they marked out a line of snow-huts with pebbles, and filled the dance-house with imaginary singers. Thus the occupations of the parents were the pastimes of the children, who learned in play their duties of after years.

Twenty-five miles west of the sand-plain, at Bad Creek, we left The Listener's wife to dry our stock of meat, promising to rejoin her before many days; with lightened packs we then pushed on toward Mt. Arrow-smith, camping near a crag of diabase twelve feet high that formed a landmark visible for many miles. Here we encountered a violent snow-storm that continued unabated for two days. We spent the first in our sleeping-bags, singing in chorus between intervals of sleep, or mocking each other's voices. Our gaiety infected even the dignified Ikpuck, who improvised a comic song about my adventure with the wolf on the Coppermine River. No hardship could quench the cheerfulness of my companions. When morning dawned, and, break-fastless, we struggled ahead in the teeth of the gale, they launched many a jest at Icehouse, who, ill-pre-pared for such inclement weather, had enveloped her portly figure in a sleeping-robe, and waddled along with the rolling gait of a bear.

The snow melted slowly, for the brief summer was drawing to its close. The last of the flowers lay withered, butterflies and moths had vanished, and even the mosquitoes had ceased their endless buzzing. The days were shortening rapidly; darkness covered the land for three hours around midnight, and on still evenings ice was forming on the ponds and lakes. It was time to retrace our steps to our caches, take down the sleds, and seek out warmer clothing. But, before turning back, we could make one brief dash to the northward and try our fortunes in the hills behind Cape Baring.

Two days later, in the unmelted snow on the slope of a ridge, we came upon the fresh tracks of two polar bears. Here was game worth the hunting. We dropped our packs on the ridge-top in charge of Icehouse and little Knife-Blade, and with three of our best dogs, tried to follow up the spoor. But the dogs could not hold to it, and, after travelling several miles from hill-top to hill-top, we turned aside to stalk a herd of caribou. The men concealed themselves behind low mounds or in hastily dug pits, and the women, going to windward of the herd, sought to drive it into the ambush; but the animals stampeded past them and fled toward the coast. The disappointed hunters followed them, while Misty, The Listener's son, and myself returned to camp to see if Icehouse had cooked our supper, for we had eaten nothing for twelve hours. Icehouse, however, had been scraping caribou skins and had neglected to gather fuel. We started a fire for her with chips from a broken walking-stick, and descended into the valley below to gather an armful of dwarf willow. Suddenly Misty shouted, and, looking up, I saw the fantastic figure of my "mother" capering and gesticulating against the sky-line. "Bears, bears!" cried Misty, recognizing the signal and dashing up the hill. We burst into the camp, exclaiming together, "Where are they? Where are they?" and Icehouse, wildly waving her arms to the north, cried, "Over there, two of them in the valley yonder." I turned my binoculars on the place and examined it carefully. She was right; two white objects were moving slowly in the distance. They could not be caribou, which had dark coats at this season; they must be the polar bears whose tracks we had seen a few hours before.

"I'll put on my boots and we'll go after them," cried Icehouse. But I answered, "The meat is almost cooked. Let us eat first and then go." The old lady was too excited to think of her cooking. "They are not caribou, are they? You can see that. There are two of them. I saw two." "Put some more wood on the fire," I said. "Oh, but look, they are coming this way. I'll take The Runner's bow and arrows, shall I?" And, unable to keep from laughing, I said, "Never mind the bears. They are a long way off. Let us have our supper." We started at last, Icehouse stumbling and panting behind us, with her son's bow slung over her shoulder. Rapidly but cautiously we climbed each intervening ridge and searched the low land beyond. One mile, two miles, three miles. Now we came in sight of the animals, this time from a nearer vantage-ground. "They are bears, aren't they?" "I don't know. They are in the water." "Look, they are moving." "Confound it, they're swans." "No." "Yes." We approached still nearer till we could doubt no longer. Our bears were only two snow-white swans floating peacefully in the centre of a lake.

The next day, when we least expected them, the bears did appear, approaching a lake on its farther side. Wild turmoil prevailed for a few minutes as we raced after the dogs to draw them under cover. The women and children guarded them behind a ridge while the men, hurrying down to the lake, lay in wait fifty yards back from the shore. Leaf, a true sportswoman, kept close to The Runner—she would not leave her husband where there was danger; and others held tightly in leash our four best dogs. As we waited, lying prone on the ground, Ikpuck and The Runner slipped off half their clothing to lighten themselves for a possible chase.

The bears entered the water and swam leisurely toward us, the cub, three-quarters grown, circling around its mother and snapping in play at her face. She fended off its attack by stretching up her neck; or she dived suddenly under, and the young one immediately followed her. They played like dogs, more at home in the water than on land; the distance across the lake was nearly a mile, but they could have swum ten miles with as little difficulty. Thus, suspecting no danger, they approached within easy range of my rifle before the old bear caught our scent and fled in terror to the opposite shore; yet even in her terror she did not forget the young one frantically swimming in her wake, but turned around from time to time to wait for it. One behind the other they dragged their unwieldy bodies out of the swampy border of the lake and disappeared at a lumbering gallop over the hill beyond.

I watched their movements through my binoculars, so fascinated by the sight that I failed to notice my companions unleash the dogs and race round the edge of the lake in hot pursuit. They, too, had almost disappeared before I wakened from my trance. I followed at top speed, stumbling half blindly up and down the ridges, and floundering through marshy tundra and shallow streams, until at the end of a three-mile steeplechase I had overtaken all except The Runner and Ikpuck, who were lost to view somewhere ahead. What direction they had taken I could not tell, so I steered for the nearest hill-top to search the countryside. Away in the distance a bear and a dog were climbing a slope, the bear in front and the dog pressing hard on its heels. The two hunters were visible nowhere, but in a small hollow not far to the right lay another bear, exhausted perhaps or sleeping. I stalked it cautiously; finger on trigger, and with heart beating loudly, I crept within a stone's throw; and still it did not move. Then I noticed red bloodstains on its flank; it was the cub, run down and shot by Ikpuck.

The dog checked the mother bear two miles ahead, where The Runner shot it with Ikpuck's rifle. The chase had ended gloriously; every one had his own story to tell about it, and every one spoke at once. To kill a bear, next to man their most formidable adversary, was the hunter's greatest glory. Ikpuck, unaided save by his dogs, had killed one two years before with a hunting-knife lashed to the end of a tent-pole. That had been a terrific battle, infinitely more thrilling than our recent chase, for what chance had the two bears against a .44 Winchester? But a bear is a bear, however it is slain, and the joy of my companions was not lessened because the danger had been slight. The species remained as formidable as ever, and its representatives, even when dead, should be treated with caution and respect. So the prudent Ikpuck placed a needle-case beside the mother, and a miniature bow and arrow beside the cub, that they might not travel empty-handed to the spirit-home of their kind.

We camped beside the carcass of the larger bear for three days, enjoying the change from venison to a heavier meat. The dogs, more starved than feasted during the last six months, gorged themselves until they could hardly move. We had meat enough to last a fortnight, yet the hunters wantonly shot three caribou, bringing in only the hides, the back fat, and the sinew. When I remonstrated against such wastefulness they merely said that caribou would always be plentiful, and that they wanted more hides to trade with their neighbours. There was one way in which I could check the slaughter, by threatening to supply no ammunition during the winter to any one who wasted the meat. The threat accomplished more than I had anticipated. They not only brought in one of the carcasses, but presented me with all the marrow-bones. More embarrassing still, Icehouse insisted on frying me the liver in back fat, as I had often done for myself; only instead of pounding the fat between two stones before she placed it in the pan, she made quite sure that it would melt by chewing it!

During our march south, Ikpuck and The Runner visited the coast to search for driftwood, returning with a fine plank that had probably washed overboard from some vessel. So unusual a prize led to considerable discussion. At first they proposed to convert it into two sled-runners, since it required less shaping than the rude logs they generally trimmed down for that purpose; but as both their sleds were in good condition they finally decided to make fish-spears, and Ikpuck split the plank carefully from end to end by means of small wedges of antler driven home with a heavy stone. He then split each section, obtaining four stout poles which he planed and smoothed with his hunting-knife. The care he expended on the task, and his manifest joy at its successful completion, made me realize the handicap under which these people laboured through the scarcity of wood in their country. If I may compare his fish-spears with a product of our own civilization, each pole had the value of a first-class magazine rifle.

All was well in our old camp at Bad Creek, where The Listener's wife had stayed to dry our meat; if anxiety or loneliness had troubled her during her nine days' solitary vigil, it certainly left no traces in her appearance or mode of greeting. Her people, unlike other Eskimo tribes, never voluntarily abandoned the aged and infirm to die of cold and starvation, but prolonged their closing years with loving care. Parents and children were united by tender bonds that neither time nor distance dissolved. I once witnessed the chance meeting of an old woman with her middle-aged son who had been living in a remote tribe for many years; the stalwart hunter knelt in the snow at her feet, and, as she raised her jacket, reverently touched with his lips the breast that had nourished him in childhood.

A little north of our camp, Bad Creek cut through an outcrop of dolomite, forming a narrow S-shaped cañon a quarter of a mile long and forty feet deep. The locality was very familiar to my companions. From a ledge just under the brow of the cliff we dropped our hooks into a deep pool, and in a few hours hauled out seven large trout. (Whether any trout remained in the pool all winter, or whether they ascended to a lake before the freeze-up, I do not know; above and below there was less than three feet of water in the stream, which would freeze to the bottom before Christmas.) A gravel beach at the outlet of the cañon contained numerous pebbles of iron pyrites, used by the natives for striking fire; and a neighbouring meadow was white with the seeds of the cotton-grass that supplied both tinder and wicks for the lamps. The women and children gathered large quantities of these seeds, stuffing them into small bags of the strangest varieties and materials. Some were worn-out stockings of squirrel or caribou fur; two were made from the membranes that had lined the hearts of our polar bears; but the most curious of all were bottle-shaped pouches sewn from the webbed feet of red-throated loons. Whatever their shape, all alike found their way into the dog-packs, where they added one more item to our varied impedimenta.

Our loads had increased considerably since those early days in August when, leaving the hills, we had commenced this ceaseless quest of caribou. Icehouse, it is true, had no longer two small puppies tearing at the back of her hair while ostensibly nestling in the hood of her jacket; they were sturdy urchins now, able to keep pace with the other dogs and to steal the meat from our packs. But in addition to her usual burden she carried fifteen pounds of tallow, her share of the caribou back fat that the women had boiled down for ease of transport. Each man had several green caribou hides rolled round his pack, and Ikpuck and The Runner bore the two bear skins, which alone weighed upward of fifty pounds. My own pack was unchanged save for two extra caribou hides, and an increase in the thickness of my herbarium from two inches to six.

Late one afternoon, as we skirted the edge of a lake, we came to an old camping-site where a woman's knife, a needle-case, and one or two smaller articles mingled with the broken poles of a tent. Although no bones were visible, we knew that some one had died here, that her spirit had gone to its "hunting-ground" with the spirits of the things she had used in life. I picked up the broken tent-poles to carry along for fuel, but laid them down again when my companions reproached me for stealing her shelter. Had I but known, I might have replaced them with miniature poles, for the dead use not the material things, but their spirits, or what we in our philosophical jargon call concepts. So, at least, Icehouse explained to me a fortnight later when, discovering another grave, she substituted a toy lamp for a real one; the deceased woman suffered no loss, and Icehouse gained a vessel of which she stood greatly in need.

It was only the second week in September, but snow that fell incessantly for three days did not melt again, and every lake was solidly bound with ice. Of birds we saw only a few ptarmigan that were already turning white, and two tiny snow-buntings which of all the migratory birds are the first to come and the last to leave. Ducks and geese, sandpipers, plovers and longspurs, all had winged their way to countries that have no winter. Many even of the ptarmigan were moving southward, and the caribou would follow them, my companions said, within the next three or four weeks. Some of the caribou herds would probably gather earlier, and wander near the coast until the freezing of the strait opened up a road to the mainland. Should we wait and intercept them, or travel north into the hills and resume our interrupted fishing? My party chose the former course, and established itself near the mouth of a large creek twelve miles west of Dryad Harbour. But Ikpuck, Icehouse, little Knife-Blade, and myself moved eastward a few miles and settled down nearer our caches.

# CHAPTER X

## DARKENING DAYS

IKPUCK chose for our tent-site a level patch of ground beside a small lake that filled a dip in the rolling plain behind Dryad Harbour. Through a hole in the ice we drew our water, and for fuel we used the dwarf willow that grew abundantly all around, or burned the yellow fat of the polar bear in a naturally hollow stone. Low ridges blocked the view on all sides, shutting out even the sea four miles away; but the ridge to the north overlooked a long valley so rich in moss that we expected the migrating caribou to make it their highway. On the crest of this ridge, therefore, we built a low semi-circular wall of stones, chinked with snow, that would both conceal and shelter the watcher; and every morning, at dawn, some one visited the look-out post to search the surrounding landscape. A conventional signal, the rapid raising and lowering of the arms, notified those in camp if caribou were visible.

For several days we roamed far and wide, finding no caribou, but innumerable traces of the hunters who had preceded us. Here were lines of stones and turf, dummy hunters like those we ourselves had erected during the summer; there were the saucer-shaped pits from which the archers had launched their arrows, and, near them, small stones, resting on larger ones, to mark the places where caribou had fallen. The marksmanship had been unerring, the toll of victims immense, if one could rely on the number of signs we encountered within the radius of a few miles; but they were no more convincing than the bullet-holes of the enemy in a trooper's hat. Even the scrupulous Ikpuck liked to set up the signs in suitable places, a small stone for a small caribou and a larger stone for a bull; he would fool the coming generations, he said. But he was not enthusiastic enough to build stone caches for all the hypothetical meat, so that a critical traveller would certainly notice the disproportion between the two marks and temper his judgment accordingly.

Disappointed at the non-appearance of the caribou, my versatile "father" sought by other means to replenish our dwindling stock of meat. He visited the harbour, where I had noticed some bearded seals playing in the open water near shore. It was not difficult to shoot them, but to bring them to land was an extremely hazardous enterprise, since a thin sheet of ice covered the water for a distance of a hundred yards out from the shore. Any dead seals that remained afloat, buoyed up by thick layers of blubber, drifted gently against its outer edge. Ikpuck crawled cautiously toward them, testing the ice in front of him with his hunting-knife; then, attaching a long line to a carcass, he retreated a few yards and dragged it out of the water. This was the most perilous task of all, and more than once the ice creaked ominously under the strain; but salt-water ice is less brittle than fresh-water, and he escaped with nothing worse than two badly frozen wrists. Out of six seals that floated he landed three, which provided enough blubber to last us a month, even if we kept the lamp burning five or six hours a day. He did not mention the freezing of his wrists, and we did not discover their condition until they turned completely black.

A lake near our camp yielded him other trophies. True trout were lacking, but salmon-trout that had migrated up from the sea earlier in the summer now began to spawn along its margin. He could see the male fish, a brilliant red at this season, swimming around little piles of boulders where the inconspicuous females deposited their eggs. They fled when his chisel struck the ice above them, but the male, and even the female, often returned, to be impaled on his long-handled fish-spear.

In the meantime I kept watch for the caribou which now showed signs of migrating. At first they came in small numbers every second or third day; but soon more frequently, until as many as fifteen or twenty passed daily near our camp. Ikpuck, giving up his sealing and fishing, joined me in the chase, and together we shot about forty animals, although we carried to camp only the hides and whatever meat we needed for immediate consumption. Some of the carcasses we cached under heavy stones, others we dropped into shallow ponds where the covering of ice would protect them from the foxes. Those that we buried under stones froze within a few hours, for the cold weather was an admirable refrigerator; and those that we submerged in the icy water preserved equally well, because the ponds were free of bacteria and too shallow for fish. We planned to recover these carcasses, of course, before the water froze to the bottom, or the ice became so thick that we could not extricate them without much labour. I earmarked twelve for the station at Bernard Harbour, where there would be no fresh meat apart from the caribou that might be shot during this migration; all the rest went to my family, who for two months longer had to live on fish and caribou alone.

Caribou, like salmon-trout, have their breeding season early in the winter. We noticed many signs of restlessness in the herds, especially in one that comprised six cows and four bulls. Three of the bulls had just reached maturity; the fourth, the leader of the herd, was a magnificent animal crowned with an enormous pair of branching antlers. It was he who guided their march as they moved quietly along, resting here and there to brush away the snow and nibble at the succulent moss beneath. His younger rivals he kept sternly in the rear, driving them back with a warning stare whenever they stole out on the flank and tried to advance to the front. Once, when he relaxed his guard, one of them pushed rapidly forward and drew the rest of the herd after him; but the leader suddenly charged, and the young upstart, declining battle, fled precipitately to his place again. Yet not always was the conflict refused; my companions had found two skeletons side by side, the antlers so closely interlocked that the embrace had been fatal to both animals.

A fortnight later, when the breeding season was at its height, the leadership was reversed. I watched two caribou, a bull and a cow, wandering alone up a deep valley, the cow in front, the bull following in her footsteps. Every instinct was subordinated to the mating impulse, so that they neither stopped to graze, nor noticed me standing in full view on the ridge above them. One behind the other, they marched slowly forward and disappeared from view at the head of the valley.

The season produced a change even in our dogs. They had lived in harmony throughout the summer, but now jealousy invaded their ranks, and nearly every day witnessed a battle. There were two ringleaders, an old dog so peaceable that we had thought him cowardly, and my good-natured team-leader Tellurak, whom I had never known to start a fight. Tellurak, unlike the other dogs, incurred no risk of injury, for the matted coat of long frizzly hair that enveloped him from head to foot, almost concealing his beady eyes, made him invulnerable to every adversary. If an unfortunate dog did pounce upon him it backed away immediately with a mass of hair between its teeth, and disturbed the camp for several hours with its violent coughs and sneezes.

Tellurak was my team-leader, from necessity only, not because of his outstanding qualities. In dogs as in men, the true leader is born, not made; training may increase his gifts, it cannot produce them. He must possess the intelligence to understand his master's commands, and the will to obey them without question; for the dog that understands, but hesitates to obey, causes more calamities than the numskull. He must be strong and brave, ready at all times to discipline his own team and to champion it against its enemies. More than all, he must possess, both in harness and out of it, a natural authority over the other dogs. Tellurak was strong and brave; he understood, partially at least, the words of command, though from sheer rascality he often disobeyed; but he had no prestige among his team-mates, and wielded less authority than the old bull caribou in the herd. Jumbo, my leader on the trip up the Coppermine River, was a dog of another calibre. In the heat of a chase he halted at my command and checked the whole team behind him; and at feeding time, when every other animal was fighting for its portion, he would quietly devour his share on the outskirts of the fray, growling away marauders twice as powerful as himself. Dogs that had not seen him before recognized his authority. He followed me once to the snow-hut of an Eskimo, whose five dogs, the fiercest in the camp, rushed out to drive him away. Jumbo stood tense, his head and tail erect, his fangs bared in a warning snarl. When they checked their wild onrush in surprise, he disdained even to glance at them, but marched haughtily through their midst into the sanctum of their home; the discomfited "huskies" (Eskimo dogs) dropped their tails and slunk in behind him. Jumbo was a born general whose authority showed in every movement; but quaint, affectionate, hard-working Tellurak should never have risen above an aide-de-camp.

The tide of migrating caribou spent itself within a

few days, and only occasional stragglers appeared in the vicinity. Our comrades to the west, who wished to inspect their caches before returning to the hills, moved over and camped beside us. But the evening after their arrival Icehouse quarrelled with The Chatterbox's wife concerning some blubber that was given to the dogs, and, after exchanging real Billingsgate, reduced her adversary to tears. Ikpuck scolded her and retired to bed. The remainder of the party soon followed his example; but when Icehouse, lingering to the last, crept in beside her husband, he sternly ordered her to sleep in an empty sealskin tent that we used for a kitchen. She protested vehemently, for a cold north wind was blowing and the thermometer nearly at zero. At a repetition of the order she began to dress, but he tore the clothes from her hands and snapped, "Get out." The poor woman, speechless with terror, fled through the tent door naked, and disappeared into the darkness. I said to Ikpuck, "Tell her to come in again. She will freeze to death." He slipped on his jacket and looked inside the cooking-tent. It was empty, nor did he know where she had gone. Five minutes later I found her in the tent of Parted-Hair's family, shivering under a spare caribou robe; but when I urged her to return she answered, "Ikpuck is too angry with me. I am afraid." I assured her that she would suffer no harm, and, returning to my sleeping-bag, told Ikpuck to drop the matter. He pretended to be sound asleep when she stole in, and the camp relapsed into silence, except that now and then a low sob issued from the tent of The Chatterbox, who had disciplined his wife by tearing her coat from top to bottom. Icehouse was unusually quiet in the morning, and our visitors departed abruptly for the hills. So once more our tent stood solitary.

In order to protect ourselves more effectively from the weather we moved into the sealskin cooking-tent, built a low rampart of turf around its base, and covered the roof with caribou hides. The small lamp that Icehouse had discovered on a grave kept our new quarters comparatively snug, and its pale, warm glow streaming through the half-open door guided us home in the darkness from our weary hunts. The weather was stormier now, the nights much longer; in a few more weeks the sun would set for its midwinter sleep. This shortness of the daylight restricted our excursions, so that we added no more than two caribou to the total we had laid aside in our caches. Sometimes we did not go hunting at all, but kept watch in turn from the look-out post and scraped caribou hides inside the tent. Icehouse made herself a pair of trousers from a skin that I scraped, and, rising at 2 A.M. a morning or two afterward, made a similar garment for me by the light of her blubber-lamp. So the days passed monotonously. At last Ikpuck decided that it was useless to stay any longer. We packed all the skins to his cache on the coast, recovered the sled that he had abandoned there in the spring, and set out for the Lake of Dancing.

At our first halting-place in the hills we found a deep snow-drift firm enough to make the perpendicular walls of a hut, but not to form its roof. By digging out and building up we contrived a circular enclosure five feet high at the floor level and six feet in diameter, exactly the size that we could cover with our summer cloth tent; and we extended its front with the sealskin tent to give Icehouse more space for cooking. Our heads almost touched the roof as we sat on the sleeping-platform, eating our supper; but the hut was so warm and cosy after the drafty tent we had occupied that we turned into our beds with every anticipation of a comfortable night. Outside the snow fell heavily, and the big soft flakes massing deeper and deeper on the roof sagged in the canvas and crushed down the walls. A feeling of oppression roused me during the early hours of the morning, and I tried to sit up, but my head came into violent contact with the ceiling before my shoulders left the bed. The shout I gave awakened the whole family; for a moment no one comprehended what had happened to us. Then Ikpuck and I, heaving together, lifted the roof a few inches, crawled off the platform, and lit the lamp. Little Knife-Blade followed us without difficulty, but the well-nourished Icehouse wriggled in her bag for several minutes before she tumbled, like an enormous chrysalis, head foremost onto the floor.

We occupied a real snow-hut at the Lake of Dancing, one that had been erected by our companions a week or more before. Here we dismantled our caches of dried meat and dried fish, and recovered my sled, the big spring tent, and all the other things we had deposited at this place in the early days of summer. Foxes, worming their way through sundry chinks and crevices in the stones, had destroyed all the sinew fishing-lines; fortunately we had plenty of cod-line that could take its place. More serious was the destruction of the white-bellied caribou hides from which Icehouse had intended to make some finely ornamented costumes for the winter dances; but I assuaged her grief by promising to purchase other hides for her when the tribes reassembled at the sealing-grounds. We sighted one of the marauding foxes near our camp, and lured it within range by squeaking like a young bird; but Ikpuck's bullet struck only the ground between its legs, and, though deluged with snow, it escaped without injury.

After fishing in various lakes for a few days with little success we overtook our companions at the source of a creek that flows into Dryad Harbour. They had abandoned all further hunting and fishing on the land under the pressure of colder weather and were returning to the coast, where they had stores of blubber to feed their lamps and give light and warmth to their houses. At this moment they were preparing their sleds for the journey, restoring the shoeing of frozen mud that had dropped off during the spring. They dug out the turf from a meadow with mattocks of curving antler, thawed and crushed it inside the houses to weed out the roots, kneaded it into "cricket-balls" with water, and plastered it along the bottoms of the upturned runners. There, while it was still soft, they moulded it into shape with their hands and scraped it smooth with long-handled knives. The mud froze to the hardness of stone, giving an admirable shoeing that would last throughout the winter; but its gritty surface required a thin coat of ice to make it friction-less against the snow, and the coat had to be renewed before each day's journey. When we were travelling down to the coast over the comparatively thin ice of a lake or river, my companions sometimes poured a few buckets of water over the surface and ran their sleds through the pool before it froze; but the usual, and, in the heart of winter, the invariable method, was to fill the mouth with water and squirt a stream over each runner, rubbing it down quickly with a mitten of polar-bear fur. The Eskimos preferred polar-bear fur because a special oil in its hair prevents the adhe-sion of water; for the same reason our zoologist-com-mander, always quick to recognize the value of Arctic products, recommended its adoption in low temperatures as a pocket-handkerchief.

Between the hills and the coast we ran into another wave of migrating caribou, the loiterers who had stayed behind in their summer pasture-grounds until the call of winter became too imperious to disobey. The strait had now frozen, but the ice was weak and dangerous, and the sky showed dark reflections from lanes of open water. No Eskimo was so foolhardy as to venture out more than three or four miles, lest a sudden gale should break the unstable field into a maze of drifting floes; yet there were tracks of caribou on the ice, all pointing south toward the mainland and none returning. My "father" told me that the old bull at the head of each herd steered a zigzag course along the edge of the thicker ice, which he tested at intervals with his forefeet. Evidently these northern caribou possess a special "ice instinct" over and above the instinct of migration; and since experience can create an instinct only when repeated through countless generations, here was definite evidence that for centuries, and even millennia, the caribou have wandered north each spring to pass the summer in the Arctic archipelagoes, and wandered south again to winter on the mainland as soon as the sea froze over in the autumn. Trespassing on unsafe ice doubtless caused many casualties during the earlier centuries of their migrations; but today the instinct seems infallible,

[ 187 ]

although a sudden storm that shatters the ice-field may still engulf a few animals before they have time to regain the shore.

The second wave of the migration passed even more quickly than the first, and we found ourselves on a barren coast, cut off from every source of food except the stores that we had accumulated during the months just past. The seals had vanished with the open water, the true fishing-lakes lay back in the hills, and the salmon-trout that Ikpuck had speared in lakes nearer the coast had either ceased to spawn, or were invisible through the crust of snow. Occasionally we sighted two or three ptarmigan, never enough for a single meal; and at the mouth of the creek, three or four feet under the ice, the children speared a few sculpins, and devoured them on the spot. But we had now reached the "doldrum" stage in our voyage, the resting period that intervenes between the intense activity of the caribou hunt and lake-fishing, and the winter sealing on the ice. So with a feeling almost of permanency we established our tiny settlement on the sea-shore, knowing that we should remain there longer than at any place since the preceding winter. We built our snow-huts with more than usual care, and the women improved them by fixing over the doorways windows of fresh-water ice chipped from a neighbouring lagoon. From morning till night they sat inside beneath their windows, sewing the new garments we needed for the winter months; as soon as they left this place for the sealing-grounds they might sew no more until the sun returned at the end of January. The men brought in the pokes of blubber cached on Read Island six months before, and the carcasses of the caribou shot during the migration just ended; in idle moments they repaired their sealing weapons or helped their wives to scrape the caribou hides.

The monotony of this new life affected the children much more than the adults. Throughout the summer they had shared our hunting and fishing, packed their burdens like the rest of us, and played an active rôle in every enterprise. They had gained a status in those months far beyond their years. Now they were reduced to children again, helpless dependents whose principal duty was to carry messages from one hut to another. Their bows and arrows, which had secured us many a duck and ptarmigan, were useless now that the birds had flown, and their fishing-lines lay idle in the family dunnage-bags, buried away until another spring. Little wonder, then, that they chafed under the confinement and tedium of a sedentary life, where no new playmates, no dances, no visitors from other tribes, breathed fresh life into our humdrum circle. A strange irritability seemed to taint their merry, care-free natures, and they wept over trifles that a month before would have passed unheeded.

Icehouse told Jennie one morning to brush the snow

from some clothes that were packed in a bag on the house-roof. Jennie refused, and petulantly turned her face to the wall. Her cousin entered the hut, and, seeing his playmate sulking in the corner, jeered at her behind her back; but a backhand that neatly struck his eye changed his jeering to a wail. The indignant Icehouse poked her daughter with a stick until she, too, added her voice to the lamentable chorus. Partnership in grief then brought comfort to both children, who left the hut together and built a common play-house in the snow outside. Pain alone could not make them weep so readily. I had seen Jennie stumble against a stone and bruise her knee so severely that she limped for two or three days; but when some one asked her if she were hurt she straightened up resentfully and marched ahead without a tear.

Even I grew restless at our inactivity. Bernard Harbour seemed so near across the strait, and for seven months I had heard no word of English, and received no news of my comrades on the expedition. In clear weather we could see the Liston and Sutton Islands on the horizon, and the station lay only twelve miles beyond. The dark streaks in the sky that reflected open water had disappeared, and a short excursion seaward revealed no wide cracks or unsafe places in the solid ice. Conditions might be different between the islands and the mainland, but Ikpuck thought that I could make the passage without danger.

I would have left him with his family, but both he and Icehouse protested. When they adopted me as their son, they said, they had promised my comrades that they would deal with me honestly, and conduct me safely back at the end of our wanderings. How, then, could Ikpuck leave me before he had landed me at the station again and proved to the white men that he had kept his word? I could not resist their argument. My "father" and I left the settlement together on the morning of November 7, and, meeting with no mishaps in our passage, arrived at Bernard Harbour the next evening.

Thus was completed the project that I had outlined for myself the previous winter. By isolating myself among the Eskimos during the months just past I had followed their wanderings day by day from autumn round to autumn. I had observed their reactions to every season, the disbanding of the tribes and their reassembling, the migrations from sea to land and from land to sea, the diversion from sealing to hunting, hunting to fishing, fishing to hunting, and then to sealing again. All these changes caused by their economic environment I had seen and studied; now, with greater knowledge of the language, I could concentrate on other phases of their life and history.

## CHAPTER XI

### THE SECOND WINTER

AN unusually large crowd greeted me as I drove my team to the station door, yet of the scientific staff of six the only representative was Johansen. Anderson, Chipman, O'Neill, and Cox were expected daily; they had gone east during the summer, and lingered too late to return except by sled. Two men were strangers, Corporal Bruce, of the Royal Northwest Mounted Police, who had been commissioned to investigate the mysterious disappearance of the Roman Catholic priests from the Dismal Lakes two years before, and Girling, a young Anglican missionary, whose schooner had been blown ashore a hundred miles west of Bernard Harbour. Among half a dozen Eskimos from the Mackenzie River delta engaged to help the expedition I recognized only the half-breed, Patsy Klengenberg, who was to be my interpreter throughout the winter.

Even the house was altered. The cache that had adjoined our single room was now transformed into a kitchen, and fitted with bunks to accommodate the cook and some of the Eskimos. It was also the dining-room, the scientists reserving the main room as a study and bedroom. The engineer installed a carbide lighting plant before Christmas to replace the kerosene lamps; and with good illumination, ample work-tables beneath the windows and rows of books above, our home seemed strangely luxurious after the simplicity of the native snow-huts. The temptation to remain there and vegetate for a time was overwhelming.

Anderson's party appeared the day after my return, and Girling left three days later to rejoin his schooner to the west. In the peace and comfort of our hut we settled down to examine our letters, and to read the sheafs of newspapers brought in from Herschel Island during the summer. April, 1914, had been the date on the last letters we had received from the outside world, and until this month of November, 1915, no rumours, not even of the Great War, had penetrated to our lonely outpost. The new mail sketched its history for nine months only, up to the beginning of May; and we held several midnight sessions speculating on the attitude of Italy, and the issues and chances of the conflict. The mail brought orders, too, for our return, now impossible until the following summer; and some of us wondered whether the war would not end before we reached civilization again and could join the contingents already in France. Fortunately, the three different nations represented in our party all favoured the cause of the Allies, and the harmony of the station remained undisturbed. But the Eskimos were troubled. Ikpuck would not believe our western natives when they told him that the white men were killing each other like caribou, and my own explanation mystified him deeply. He pondered the subject for some days, wondering whether, after all, the ancient traditions of his people might not be true; certainly white men who deliberately used their extraordinary knowledge and powers for the wholesale massacre of each other were strangely unnatural and inhuman.

Exciting as was our mail, it did not interfere with the regular duties at the station. Johansen had made some tidal observations during the early summer. To supplement them we built a snow-house on the ice outside the harbour, dug a hole through its floor, and for two weeks measured the depth of the water every half-hour by means of a graduated rod. The day was divided into four periods of four hours each, with one long period from midnight to 8 A.M.; and each man undertook a watch in rotation. The hut was nearly a mile from the station, hidden from view by the small island that masked the entrance to the harbour. No one could lose his way by day; but at night, with no guide save the stars (if they happened to be visible), the relief man had to reach the low crest of the island before he could see the light of the lantern shining mistily through the hut's snow wall. So when Anderson left the station one evening to take over the watch from Chipman, and an hour passed without the latter's return, we became a little anxious. Then two rifle-shots suddenly echoed in quick succession from the ice, and some Eskimos shouted that a polar bear had attacked Chipman at his lonely post. The station turned out in a tumult. Some of us rushed to the tide-hut, only to find him standing outside, wondering at the lanterns that gleamed on every side, at the two rifle-shots, and at Anderson's mysterious absence. More anxious still, we scattered over the ice to search for Anderson, and at last saw him approaching, safe and unharmed. He had sighted what he thought was the tide-hut lantern soon after he left the station, but, though he hastened forward, it seemed to draw no nearer. Finally he realized that his beacon was a solitary star that shone mistily low down on the horizon. He was alone far out on the ice of the strait; the tide-hut and the station lay somewhere in the darkness behind him. Hoping for an answering signal he fired his rifle, and the imagination of an Eskimo supplied the missing tragedy.

Eskimos from both sides of the strait, and from the Coppermine River area, flocked to the station to trade before the opening of the sealing season, until their new-born village on the edge of the ice contained nearly a hundred and fifty inhabitants. They remained with us for three weeks, giving no trouble, although we excluded all but Ikpuck's family from the house until nightfall. I tried, with Patsy's assistance, to delve into their religion and to record their ancient traditions; but privacy was impossible and fear of public disapproval sealed their lips. They spent their days in trading with me, or in visiting each other's huts and holding impromptu dances; then, after the white men had put away their note-books and retired to read in their bunks, they gathered around my phonograph and filled the house with song. Although the love of music is inborn, not taught, I had hoped that the sweetness of their voices would kindle an æsthetic glow in the cold, scientific breasts of my companions. But Cox leaped violently from his bed one midnight, and with neither sympathy nor ceremony expelled the belated choristers into the outer darkness.

All the chants they sang for me were either dance-songs or incantations to create fine weather. I asked them for lullabies; they responded with more dance-songs. The mother who rocked her baby to sleep on her back, under the warm fur coat, crooned the same melodies that she shouted in the dance-house to the booming of the drum. Were there no war-songs, no chants of victory? They asked me what war meant, for they knew of no enemies except the Indians far to the south, whom they seldom saw and carefully avoided. Surely, then, there were love-songs, songs in which the youth declared his passion and praised his fair one's beauty. No, life was hard, marriage a necessity for all. The maiden must wed a hunter who could provide her with food, clothing, and shelter, and the youth must seek out a bride who would prepare his food and sew his garments. If couples failed to agree, they could separate and find other mates. Beauty, that soon faded, did not help them in the struggle for life's necessities, and romance was stifled. The dance-house was the social hearth. There they chanted their prayers to the mystic powers that controlled the weather, that could shatter the ice-fields or withhold the game; and there, in song, they narrated their adventures and retailed the news from distant tribes. The incantations were their prayers, the dance-songs their chronicle of current events. Ikpuck sang of our polar-bear hunt, and song and story spread far along the coast, growing more garbled and unintelligible at every stage of their journey. The words of his song mattered little; every dancer could improvise new syllables, like the foreigner who sings Italian opera. What counted most was the new melody, bringing joy to the hearts of a people who found in music their highest relief from the gloom and perils of the long Arctic night. Nature, when she condemned them to this twilight land, granted them the gift of song, and, however harsh their voices, their melodies revealed a deep sense of musical beauty. The example given below was transcribed unchanged from one of my phonograph records, and only the harmonies added to adapt it to the pianoforte.

The natives moved away at last to the Liston and Sutton Islands, whither Patsy and I followed them; but we returned to the station for Christmas, accompanied by Jennie and another child. Our party had grown from nine the previous winter to seventeen, half of whom were Eskimo assistants from the west. Mainly for their pleasure we set up a Christmas tree, filled their stockings with presents, and held sports in the snow outside the station house. Patsy contributed an unexpected item to the program of events. He carved the figure of a bird from a snow-block, and caused a stampede for shotguns and .22 rifles by abruptly announcing that a ptarmigan had settled at our door; three men levelled their guns at the dummy bird before the trick was discovered. With presents and games the fête succeeded gloriously, and the cook rounded it off with a Christmas dinner that included real mince pies and an enormous plum pudding. Through it all little Jennie and her playmate wandered about in a daze, neither comprehending our strange actions, nor the

# DANCE SONG

Arr. by Marion Bauer

meaning of the flags and tinselled paper that covered the walls and tables of our hut. But when they opened their "stockings," filled to the brim with chocolate cakes, needles, thread, and enough cloth to make each of them a dress, their eyes nearly burst from their sockets and their joy pealed forth in uncontrollable laughter.

Guests are indispensable for a perfect Christmas, and ours, though unheralded, were none the less welcome. Two half-civilized Eskimos and their wives from the hinterland of Hudson Bay, hearing that white men had settled in Dolphin and Union Strait, journeyed four hundred miles to visit us and to barter their furs for ammunition, tea, and tobacco. They arrived two days before Christmas, and left us the day following it to return to their country; but on Christmas evening they thanked us for our hospitality by holding a dance in the kitchen. The only drum we could muster was an aluminum frying-pan with a hard, penetrating note, which our visitors pounded nobly as they pranced round the room, chanting a monotonous refrain. Jennie and her companion thought the music rather strange, and seemed relieved when the concert ended. As for ourselves, while we greatly appreciated the goodwill of our guests, we kept the door wide open and expedited their retirement with a liberal present of tobacco.

After Christmas, Patsy and I returned to the Eskimos at the Liston and Sutton Islands on a day when the calm weather had drawn every hunter out to the ice-field, even women and young boys. They were standing like pillars over their individual seal-holes, scarcely daring to raise their heads lest they should alarm the seals beneath. But one hunter, Big-Tooth, hailed us, and thinking that he might have harpooned a large bearded seal which he was unable to draw up alone, I sent Patsy ahead with the sled, and hastened to his assistance. As I drew near, however, he left the seal-hole and sauntered toward me.

"It's the white man," he called.

"Yes, Big-Tooth."

"I've had no luck with my sealing," he continued.

"Is that so?"

"Ikpuck has been very successful."

"That's good news."

"I'll search around a little longer before I go home."

"Very well. I'm going straight to the camp." With these words I moved away, but he called out again:

"By the way, have any of our eastern kinsmen arrived yet?"

"No, not yet," I answered, and moved on a few yards.

"By the way, I'll be going home soon."

"Oh, very well," I called without halting.

"By the way, if I catch a seal will you give me some cartridges for part of the meat?"

"Perhaps."

"You can use it for dog-food, you know."

"Yes." And I continued on.

"By the way, I'm Big-Tooth, you know."

"Yes, Big-Tooth."

"By the way—". But I pretended not to hear him and hurried to overtake Patsy. Big-Tooth was a good fellow and deservedly popular; yet even his countrymen, whose own minds moved in constant circles round the material present, took to flight whenever he joined in a conversation.

On reaching the islands we erected a tent inside an unusually large snow-hut that opened into Ikpuck's dwelling. This was an admirable arrangement for two reasons; the hut gave us shelter from the wind, and the tent made it possible to set up a stove where we could burn some of the driftwood that lined the western beaches of the island. Here, with more privacy, we made another attempt to investigate the mythology and religion of the people. Ikpuck and Icehouse gladly told us all they knew, and though not well versed in the traditional lore of their people, they could direct us to better informants. We then closeted ourselves with two old men, whose hearts we warmed with some hard biscuits and cups of steaming chocolate. The comfortable tent and the unusual beverage loosened their tongues, and when one man

lifted the veil of secrecy a few inches the other raised
it higher, lest silence should rob him of a share in the
reward. In the end it was not their secretiveness that
hampered our researches, but our ignorance of their
ways of thought and their own inability to narrate
a story from the ground upward; for they invariably
began with the crisis, so to speak, and worked backward and forward, with many omissions and repeti-
tions, on the tacit assumption that our minds moved
in the same groove as theirs and that explanations
were needless.

If the preceding winter had been unusually mild,
this one was unusually stormy. Gales from east and
west—the two prevailing quarters—swept the shelter-
less ice-field day after day until its covering of snow
grew hard like a macadamized road. Then the wind
blew narrow furrows along it, *sulci* with crests so
sharp that they hurt the feet. Hunters who ventured
out to seal could find no breathing-holes amid the
driving snow, and with difficulty reached their homes
again. The first gales passed unheeded. The people
had fish and caribou meat stored outside their huts,
and pokes of blubber for their lamps. Gathered inside
the dance-house, they could laugh at the howling blizzards and while away the hours in song and gymnas-
tics. But when their food was exhausted, when half
their lamps had expired from want of oil, dance-songs

gave place to incantations, and shaman after shaman sent forth his spirit to seek the dread sea-goddess at the bottom of the ocean and force her to relent. Temporary lulls in the storms drove every hunter to the sealing-grounds; on calm days they left the settlement two or three hours before dawn and returned in the darkness. As the dogs dragged the booty into the passageways the children threw themselves on the seal carcasses and poured water into their mouths to please their spirits and induce other seals to rise to the hunters' harpoons. Dolphin and Union Strait was one of the richest sealing-grounds along the Arctic coast, and the natives with whom we camped escaped any dire privations this winter; but in Coronation Gulf, as we learned afterward, many Eskimos ate the sealskin covers of their bows, and some old people perished through the hardships they were compelled to endure.

The storms were responsible for other tragedies. A boy of about six years, the only son of a strange, priest-like individual whom we knew as "The Prophet," was blown from the roof of a snow-hut during a gale, breaking his thigh just above the knee. The father, aided by an elderly medicine-man, set the leg in short splints bound round with a caribou hide. As soon as I heard of the accident I offered to take the lad to our station, where we would care for him until he could walk again; and the parents, who had often been our guests, gratefully accepted, on condition that the old medicine-man also gave his consent. When I asked them why they needed the medicine-man's permission they told me that he had undertaken to effect a cure, provided he were given the boy in payment; and that they had consented, much against their will, lest the child should be crippled for life. They requested the old man to release them from the engagement, but he refused, not unnaturally, perhaps, since he hoped that the boy would support him in his declining years; and the parents dared not go back on their word for fear of the old man's witchcraft. So the boy did not return with me, but remained in the settlement; and though his leg healed rapidly, his family lost him for ever.

Fate dealt less harshly with Fish-Head, a kindly old simpleton who harboured no ill-will toward any one. He had bought from me a .44 Winchester rifle, which he lashed inside a sealskin and stored at the back of his sleeping-platform. Knife, the shrewd medicine-man who had acquitted me of murder, told him that the weapon would rust inside the hut, and advised him to keep it on the parapet among the bales of clothing. Two nights after the old man changed its position the rifle disappeared. No one, of course, had stolen it; all the people accepted Knife's explanation,

that the dogs had dragged it away in the darkness
and the drifting snow had concealed it from sight.
The distracted owner came to me: Could I not find
it was the magic needle that spun round and round
when I placed my knife beneath it, but at rest always
pointed in the same direction? I listened to his story
attentively, and promised that he should recover the
rifle before many days. That same evening I was
visited by Knife, who also owned a .44 Winchester
rifle, which I had agreed to replace with a more powerful 30.30 if he taught me the lore of his people. After
mentioning Fish-Head's misfortune, I said: "You
must be able to find his weapon, for you are the
greatest medicine-man in this country. See that it
is given back to him, for until it is found I can neither
change your own rifle nor trade with any of your
people." He protested vehemently against such an
impossible task, and when I would not relent, departed
in ill-humour. Nothing happened for two days; Knife
kept aloof from me, and I abstained from all trade.
Then one stormy morning an excited crowd broke into
my tent, led by the triumphant Fish-Head. The rifle
was found. Knife, the great medicine-man, had discovered it. He had gone out to shoot a raven that
haunted the settlement, although the people had never
thought of harming it before, and had come upon the
rifle half buried in the snow. Knife himself stood

grinning in the background. I congratulated him; he *was* a great medicine-man. And later I changed his own .44 rifle for a 30.30.

A woman who entered Ikpuck's hut about 4 A.M. one morning, announced that his half-niece had just given birth to a daughter. Icehouse dressed quickly and went over to visit the mother; but Ikpuck, after the first enquiries, paid no further attention. A boy would have augmented the ranks of the hunters; but a girl, well, she was only one more to support. I, too, gave the matter no thought, leaving at day-break to return to the station. But the day following the newly delivered wife and her husband marched across the strait in the teeth of a blizzard and built a snow-hut beside us. The baby remained behind. It had come at an inopportune season when the parents were migrating to the eastward; so without a pang they had crushed out its little life and laid the body on the wind-swept snow.

Four other mothers destroyed their babes this winter within an hour of delivery. Terrible as their crime may seem, they should not be condemned too hastily. Every society has devised some method, conscious or unconscious, for checking the full and unrestricted growth of its population; and infanticide, the simplest of them all, was in past ages the most widely spread. Greece and Rome condoned it, and even

Christianity with its emphasis on the value of the individual soul has failed to eradicate it entirely in civilized countries. The Eskimos knew nothing of obstetrics or "child welfare," nothing of any branch of medicine; and the mother received little consideration, according to our standards, before and after her child was born. Instead of resting quietly at home, relieved of her heaviest duties and concentrating on the care of her babe, she performed all her usual tasks up to the moment of parturition, and resumed them within a few hours of delivery. Until the child gained strength to walk alone she carried it everywhere on her back, from morning till night, except when a brief respite from work permitted her to lay it among the bed-skins and personally watch over its safety; the ravenous dogs would make short shrift of an infant left unguarded within the hut or tent. On long winter marches she sometimes wrapped it in warm caribou robes and lashed it on top of the sled; but in summer it rode on her back-pack, which was not lightened in any way to compensate for the additional load. Then there was its food. Cow's milk and cereals did not exist for these Eskimos, and no babe could survive on fish and flesh, the only foods the country yielded. When the child began to walk it might swallow a morsel or two of seal or caribou meat well masticated by the parents, but for three years and even longer the mother furnished its nourishment from her own breast. Can we blame her if sometimes she shrank from the burden? Often she had no choice. It was physically impossible for her to raise twins, or children born within two years of one another; and there were no hospitals or infants' homes to which she could turn for aid. Surely it was kinder to stifle the infant in its first hour of extra-uterine life, before it knew pain or hunger, or could awaken by its cries and smiles the tender love that as yet lay sleeping in the mother's heart!

Life was so full of hardships and dangers that the average expectation was low. The young might laugh and play their innocent games, but the days passed quickly and the Great Dark was never far remote. Often, as we planned for the months to come, Ikpuck or Icehouse added in a tone of resignation, "If we still live." What lay beyond the Darkness no one knew. Even the legends contradicted one another; one version proclaimed that the dead had their home in the moon, another that they haunted this lower world, though invisible to human eyes. Whatever their fate, it held no promise of joy, no hope of reunion with kinsmen who had gone before. The only pleasures were here and now, and the wise man grasped them before they passed from his reach for ever. Death, when it beckoned, he faced with equanimity; if it deprived him of further pleasures, it also released him from manifold pains. So the Eskimos conceived no harm either to themselves or to the babe in quenching its new-born life, whenever that life seemed destined to bring only hardship and distress.

Life was sweet, nevertheless, and the natives did not desire the suicide of their race. They needed children for their own happiness, to satisfy the instinct for parenthood and to support their declining years; but they needed no more than would maintain their number at an even level. Many mouths were hard to feed; even with their number limited as at present people starved to death at intervals of a few years. To migrate elsewhere was useless, for no country between the four pillars that held up the sky abounded more in fish and game than their own. The best hunter could hardly raise more than three children, unless indeed he was fortunate enough to secure a rifle and ammunition from the white men, and thereby increase his kill of caribou and seal. Perhaps, if they all possessed rifles, they could allow their families to increase. But with only harpoons for seals, and only bows and arrows for caribou, how could they possibly provide for every child that, wanted or unwanted, now came into the light of day?

Girling, the missionary, arrived at the station early in February. This was his first winter in the country where he had undertaken to remain five years; and of the Eskimos and their customs he knew nothing. Although he had brought a Christian Eskimo from Alaska as interpreter he realized that he could accomplish little until he himself learned the language and understood the thoughts of the people. The interpreter was faithful and diligent, but unable to distinguish the essentials of Christianity from its trappings, so that his zeal sometimes outran his master's wishes. On his first Sunday at the Liston and Sutton Islands, before he was even acquainted with the people, he prohibited all sealing and sewing; consequently Icehouse objected to stitching a small rent in my mitten, saying that their own medicine-men often prohibited sewing when danger threatened, and that surely I did not wish to expose her to grave peril at the hands of some unknown but malignant power. I have no doubt that Girling believed in the proper observance of one day in seven, but it was not the first instruction he would have given to natives ignorant of a Supreme Deity, and with no word in their language for any number above six. A missionary should walk warily and circumspectly; before all else he should gain the confidence of his people, learn to speak their tongue, and understand the problems of their daily life. Girling had already begun this task. He was studying the language in every spare moment, and he visited with me all the natives who frequented Dolphin and Union Strait. Now, to extend his observations, he asked that he might accompany me on a trip to the eastward, where I proposed to make a reconnaissance of all the tribes from the Coppermine River to Kent Peninsula.

# CHAPTER XII

## THROUGH BLIZZARDS TO SPRING

**A**BURNING passion was inflaming the heart of The Runner, Icehouse's son. He craved for a Winchester rifle, like the .44 he had used so successfully against the polar bear; and he offered me anything he owned in exchange for one. If he could not earn it by teaching me the native traditions, of which he knew too little, he could at least guide me to the eastern natives, introduce me to them as his adopted brother, and in that way help my researches. His wife, Leaf, pleaded in his favour; but she made me promise, quite unnecessarily as it happened, that I would protect him from the wiles of the women in the

[ 213 ]

Musk-ox land and restore him without delay, whole in body and untouched in heart. "Men are so foolish with women," she added, noting his tolerant smile.

Four of us, then, The Runner, Girling, Patsy, and myself, piled our belongings upon a sled and turned our faces eastward. Close to Locker Point, we reached a village of the Coppermine River natives, where signs of starvation confronted us on every side. The women, sheltered behind low walls of snow, were fishing for tom-cod to replace the seals their husbands could not catch; the lamps burned low in many of the huts, or were extinguished from lack of oil; and the hungry children gathered round our tent to beg for food. During the two days we stayed in their village we invited as many as we could to share our meals; but when they uncovered our sled in the darkness, broke into a box of hard biscuits, and emptied twenty-five pounds of rice into their mittens, we brushed the snow of their settlement from our shoes and resumed the interrupted march.

Our next stopping-place was a small settlement near the mouth of Tree River, a hundred miles farther east. The inhabitants turned out as usual to greet us, and after the first salutations, an elderly man, who appeared to be the leader of the band, invited us to enter his hut. There his daughter, a young woman about twenty years of age, was skilfully flensing a freshly killed seal. Her greasy clothes, dishevelled hair, gory arms, and

face besmirched with blood and blubber from the tit-
bits she slipped into her mouth, made a somewhat
unattractive picture to our European eyes, though
the Eskimos thought it charmingly homelike. But as
soon as she finished her task she washed with snow,
dried her face and hands with a ptarmigan skin,
braided her hair, and changed into a neat suit of brown
caribou fur adorned with red and white insertion. In
this new setting she shone with quite a different
radiance; for her face, though almost circular, was so
regular, and her complexion so fresh and clear, that
even the blue tattoo lines with which all the Eskimo
women in this country marred their faces only added
piquancy to her charms. If Girling had consented to
carry out his missionary duties we would certainly have
christened her the "Boreal Venus."

These natives had been in close contact with Anderson's party during the summer and regarded all white
men with the greatest respect. When they learned
that we intended to stay with them for a few days they
renovated an empty hut for our use and equipped it
with a stone lamp, which the women supplied with oil
and tended night and morning. They, too, like the
people we had just left, had suffered from starvation
for several weeks; but now their hunters were killing
more seals, and as the days lengthened they looked confidently forward to a season of plenty. Their leader
and his wife almost embarrassed us with hospitality.

We visited him every evening, listened to his adventures at the sealing-ground, watched him re-enact each little drama inside the hut, and brandish his harpoon over imaginary seal-holes. His wife overhauled our clothing, and placed our hut on her distribution list for a daily ration of meat. Day or night, they welcomed us in their home like their own children, and—what gave us the most pleasure—looked for no recompense; indeed, they seemed quite surprised when at parting we offered them a few small gifts from our scanty store.

Several miles east of their settlement was a pyramid four feet square at the base and twelve feet high, built of flattish slabs of limestone and sandstone interspersed with boulders of diabase and granite. A vertical slab of limestone rather more than a foot long, that projected above a horizontal one three times that length, formed at the top a cross visible from a distance of three or four miles. The Runner told us that white travellers had constructed the monument long before he was born—Sir George Simpson's people, we discovered later, when they were weather-bound in this place in 1839. If they left any other record of their visit it was concealed inside the pyramid, which, of course, we did not dismantle; but wedged between two of the outer stones was a board from a biscuit box stamped "Canadian Arctic Expedition," with a date, "September, 1915," written in pencil underneath.

Being sorely in need of kindling we carried away the board on our sled, and congratulated ourselves on not having to cut shavings of wet driftwood at the end of the day's march, when our fingers were always freezing from cold and exhaustion. The matter passed entirely from my memory, along with other trivial incidents of the journey, until it was mentioned at the station a few weeks later. Then the storm of indignation that burst over my head dumbfounded me. Whose, after all, was the greater vandalism? Mine to destroy with fire the record of my enterprising colleagues, or theirs to mar with an unseemly biscuit box the enduring monument of a gallant explorer?

From the monument we struck north-east until we came to a deserted village of forty snow-huts, representing a population of perhaps 140. The inhabitants had divided into two bands, one travelling north-east, the other north-west, to different sealing-grounds. We followed the latter's sled-trails, partly because they were more numerous, partly also to escape the east wind against which we had struggled all the way from Bernard Harbour. Not a soul was visible as we drove up to the new village through the driving snow; even the dogs, drowsing in the passageways, failed to notice our arrival. The Runner shouted and disappeared into the first hut, to emerge a moment later with a smiling youth whom he introduced to me as his brother. Then the dogs began to howl, people came tumbling out from all directions, and the whole band of the Musk-ox tribe surrounded us, every household vying with the others in offering us hospitality. Girling went to one house, Patsy and I to another, and The Runner lodged with his brother.

This "brother" puzzled me. If Icehouse had only one son, as I had always understood, why did The Runner call the man his brother? Of course, he might be an adopted son like myself, but the Eskimos usually distinguished an adopted kinsman by adding a special suffix to the term of relationship. The mystery was soon explained. A quarter of a century earlier Icehouse's first husband had met the young man's father in this region and established a permanent relationship with him by a temporary exchange of wives. Although the youth was not born until three or four years afterward, The Runner considered him a true brother from whom he could claim all a brother's rights and privileges; and I, though a stranger and a white man, was his adopted brother, with a similar claim to his friendship and help.

When the villagers gathered for a dance that evening The Runner found still another connection. A Musk-ox man and his wife hailed him as their "dancing-companion," declaring that he had filled that rôle for them many years before when they were visiting Dolphin and Union Strait. In virtue of this relationship they claimed the right to extend the village's official welcome, and danced in front of him, interspersing their songs with impromptu speeches to express their delight at his visit. The Runner, who had the prerogative of dancing next, made a suitable reply, saying how glad he had been to accompany his "white brother" on this journey and to meet once more his old acquaintances of the Musk-ox land. The whole ceremony resembled the joyous reunion of long-separated friends. As he remarked to me afterward, when the gathering dispersed, "It is good to establish dancing-companions in every tribe, for then you are sure of a welcome wherever you travel."

The cheerfulness of the villagers amid their hardships aroused our admiration. On Victoria Island the Eskimos with whom I had wandered frequently fasted for twenty-four and even forty-eight hours. The experience was no novelty in their lives; they merely tightened their belts, trudged steadily forward a dozen or fifteen miles, and said smilingly, "If we sight no caribou today we will tomorrow; or, if not tomorrow, certainly the day after." It was summer then, and our tents were comfortable even without fires. But in this village the winter gales were raging, the temperature fluctuating between 25 and 45 degrees below zero Fahrenheit, and ill-luck had been trailing the natives for several weeks. The hunters had searched for seals in the fiercest blizzards until every man's face was scarred with frost-bites, but the number they had captured hardly sufficed to keep them alive. Now their strength was impaired by starvation, their huts cold from lack of oil in the lamps. One or two families, driven by hunger, had even eaten the dry sealskin cases of their bows. Perhaps it was the nearness of spring that buoyed up their courage, for none of them showed despondency or gloom, despite their pinched faces and empty cooking-pots. Indeed, they seemed more distressed by their apparent inhospitality, for several of our visitors apologized at being unable to offer us the usual presents of meat.

We stayed with them three days, and each morning the men left early for their hunting-grounds, although, half blinded by the snow-clouds, they could find few seal-holes and captured not a single seal. Our own supplies were running dangerously low; we had full rations for three days only, and the return journey to Bernard Harbour required at least a week. So we reloaded our sled and struck southward to the mainland, hoping to find game of some description as we skirted the coast.

Our departure marked the beginning of even worse weather, for the temperature dropped lower still, and the wind, which had blown in our faces throughout the eastward march, now swung round to smite us from the west. That first day's journey to the mainland tried us all severely, and though I perhaps suffered most—my health being far from good at this period—

my companions, too, found it difficult to keep their cheeks and noses from freezing. We reached land about four o'clock in the afternoon, and set up the tent beside the first stick of driftwood that was large enough to start a fire. I asked Girling, who was nearly as exhausted as myself, to arrange the boxes and sleeping-gear while the rest of us scoured the beach for more wood; but while I was setting up the stove inside the tent the three men started up the dogs and stole away. It was useless to follow them; I lit the fire, melted some snow in our largest cooking-pot, arranged the tent, and waited.

They were absent about two hours, and brought back, not merely wood, but a caribou. This was an unexpected godsend. We had counted on killing three or four hares, and perhaps a brace of ptarmigan, but not a caribou, for in early March the herds were usually far inland, just beginning their northward migration. This animal had probably strayed from a herd that had wintered near the coast, like those we had seen the winter before on the Coppermine River. But whatever the explanation, it gave us no concern at the moment; our only interest was in the meat, which tided us over a rather serious emergency.

Girling described the hunt very graphically. He and Patsy, having left their rifles behind, remained with the sled while The Runner stalked the animal from inland. The bullet struck its flank, and it fled down the slope to the ice apparently unwounded. Patsy, whipping out his knife, cut the trace of the leading dog, which dashed away in pursuit; the rest of the team followed, and Girling and Patsy flung themselves on the sled as it swept by. Caribou, dog, and dog-team raced wildly over the sea-ice; and down the cliff raced The Runner, his hood thrown back over his head and his mittens lying forgotten in the snow. The free dog caught the caribou by the throat and dragged it to its knees. Then the team came up, and Patsy, leaping from the sled, jumped on the animal's back and plunged his knife into its heart. So the chase ended. The only casualties were the caribou and The Runner, who froze his forehead, cheeks, and wrists in the excitement of the pursuit.

The remainder of our journey to the station was a weary struggle against a cold head wind and driving snow. An unusually violent gale detained us two nights on an islet, and both the dogs and ourselves were reduced to half-rations for the last four days, but no one mentioned the deficiency except Patsy. Being a very energetic hunter, he generally paralleled our course to one side in order to scour the islands and coast-line for game. It happened that on two evenings he failed to overtake us before we had pitched camp and eaten our supper; and on each occasion he angrily reproached us for leaving him *more* than his share, as he thought, of the scanty repast.

Spring came suddenly about the middle of March, when the thermometer rose well above zero. Our station then became the Mecca for tribes from as far east as the Musk-ox people, who, like the nearer Eskimos, clamoured for trade goods, rifles, and ammunition. These were not the people I had visited three or four weeks previously, but kinsmen from the second camp a few miles farther east, who had lingered at their new sealing-ground until milder weather enabled them to undertake the long journey to Bernard Harbour without hardship. Their leader was a short, white-bearded medicine-man, brusque but always dignified in his movements, and with a shrewd, kindly face that attracted immediate attention. Undoubtedly he possessed great force of character, for his tribesmen reverenced him as a father and complied with all his wishes; nominally the Eskimos recognize no chiefs among themselves, considering every man the equal of every other.

The old man taught me some of his ancient lore, and even summoned a familiar spirit that I might record a shamanistic séance on the phonograph. His followers credited him with the most fantastic powers; he could fly through the air like a bird, go down into the ocean like a fish, see what was happening hundreds of miles away. But the old man never boasted of these things; they might be true, he said, and they might not, for he lost all consciousness of himself when the familiar spirits took possession of his body. We listened to their stories courteously but incredulously, for we had heard similar tales of other medicine-men; and when he quietly informed us one morning that something was wrong with our schooner, that the thing which made it go had broken during the night, we paid no attention. What could he know about the vessel or its engine, since he had never seen a schooner before, nor indeed any boat that moved under sails or power? Yet that same afternoon we discovered a serious crack in the rafter supporting the roof of our kitchen, and the rafter was the schooner's jib-boom! Was it merely coincidence, I wonder, or did the old man really possess some uncanny power of which we, for all our vaunted knowledge, were ignorant?

As the days grew longer and the air warmer, the harbour became more deserted. Cox and O'Neill had already gone eastward to continue their survey of the coast, Anderson and Chipman had gone west to examine the Crocker River, and Johansen was exploring the south coast of Victoria Island. The Musk-ox people returned to their home, and the local natives began to separate into small bands and move toward different hunting-grounds.

Suddenly a case of ammunition disappeared, and the handful of natives who lingered beside us disclaimed all knowledge of the theft. Our old friend Knife could have enlightened us, for he always kept abreast of any mischief that was afoot; but his lips appeared sealed. The affair clearly called for strategy. In the quiet of the evening Girling and I critically compared rifles until the inquisitive Knife, drawn more and more into the discussion, rushed off at last to bring his own Winchester for a similar inspection. With his rifle securely in our hands we sprang the trap; we would not return it until he informed. The rascal scarcely hesitated; he not only revealed the name of the thief, but offered to guide us to his camp, since the man had already moved away toward Victoria Island. Morning saw our new ally running ahead of the dog-team, setting the course, while Girling and I, armed with automatics, trotted steadily in the rear, gripping the handle-bars of the sled.

All the men in the thief's village were absent at the sealing-ground when we halted our team, and only women and children had charge of the camp. We ransacked his tent inside and out, amid voluble protests from the outraged wife, who planted herself in front of each bag and tried to prevent its examination; her outcries subsided into an uneasy muttering when we uncovered thirty small boxes of the missing cartridges. Unable to find the remaining twenty we decided to await the thief himself, and deposited his bow and arrows on our sled to aid his memory.

After some hours an old man appeared in the distance, preceded by two dogs dragging a seal. The women hurried forward in a body to warn him of the hold-up, but he sent them back to their tents and approached us with a friendly greeting. "Remain quietly beside your sled," he said. "I will intercept each hunter as he comes in and counsel him to put away his harpoon. If the men have only knives in their hands there will be less danger of violence."

We thanked him for the advice, and waited quietly while the hunters planted their weapons in the snow outside the tents and gathered beside us. By chance or good fortune the thief arrived last. We advanced to meet him, all except the worthy Knife, who prudently mounted the sled well away from the scene of action that he might shout and gesticulate in perfect safety. The thief stopped short in his tracks, a look of terror spread over his face, and he rushed toward his tent, expecting instant death. Intercepted on every side, he struggled desperately until his strength failed; then, amazed to find himself still unharmed, he calmed down and showed us the hiding-place of seven more boxes. The rest he had given to a Coppermine River native who had moved so far away that we thought it hardly worth our while to pursue him.

This issue of the matter satisfied everyone. The thief, who received back his bow and arrows, escaped more lightly perhaps than he deserved, certainly more lightly than if he had robbed his own countrymen. But there were mitigating circumstances that pleaded in his favour. We were foreigners in their land, beings partly of another world, who were blessed with many wonderful things that the Eskimos lacked. Though kindly enough after our own peculiar fashion, we neither observed their customs concerning the sharing of food with neighbours, nor assumed the other obligations of their semi-communistic life. If we thus claimed exemption from the only social code they knew, could we fairly expect them to observe their moral code toward us, and regard our property as inviolate? It speaks highly of their character that nearly all of them did observe it, and not only dealt with us honestly, but reproved those of their countrymen who deviated from the accepted path. We had come to this camp prepared for serious trouble, but the goodwill of its inhabitants, prudently directed by the old man, relieved the situation of all danger.

Spring was now fast advancing, the surface of the snow was beginning to thaw under the noon sun, and the night was almost as bright as the day. Girling considered that it was time for him to go back to his vessel a hundred and fifty miles to the west, that he might sail into Bernard Harbour and establish his mission there as soon as the ice broke up in the strait. I offered to escort him, since the interpreter and dog-team he had brought to our station during the winter had long since returned. The trip would be only a pleasure jaunt at this season, and I could search the coast-line for the ruins of ancient habitations.

The journey, outward and return, lasted three weeks, for we travelled leisurely, enjoying to the full the clear atmosphere and bright, warm sunshine that had succeeded the winter blizzards and cold. Patches of bare ground here and there relieved the monotony of the white snow, the chirping of spring birds filled the air, and numerous seals basked on the surface of the ice outside their breathing-holes. We saw several tent-rings near the shore, and an arrow and other objects lying beside two human skulls, grim relics of a forgotten tragedy. But what intrigued us most was the discovery of three stumps, rotted almost to ground level, that indicated quite clearly the site of an exceedingly ancient house.

All the Eskimo tribes in the western Arctic, where the coast-line is littered with large spruce and cotton-wood trees brought down by the Mackenzie and Yukon Rivers, dwell in houses built of wood. But driftwood is so scarce in the Coronation Gulf area that the natives often made long journeys overland to distant forests in the interior in order to obtain even the small amount of timber required for sleds and narrow tables. Their only fixed dwellings were the huts of snow with which we had become so familiar; houses built wholly or partly of wood were entirely outside their knowledge. Even their traditions failed to record such houses, although they mentioned huts of stone, still standing in certain places, that a race of dwarfs had built in earlier days. Could it be that the natives had simply forgotten the customs of their forefathers, or was this wooden house in their country a relic of some ancient tribe that had either moved westward or become extinct?

Many small differences between the Eskimos here and their kinsmen in the Mackenzie River delta spoke in favour of the second theory. The Coronation Gulf people possessed no large open boats such as the western natives used for travelling along the coast, and they never employed the one-man canoes or kayaks for hunting seals. Their tools and weapons were much less varied, their clothing of different pattern, and their skill in carving greatly inferior. Altogether their culture seemed less developed than that of the western Eskimos, although the people themselves were not inferior in intelligence.

A year later Girling excavated a wooden house close to the ruin we had discovered on this journey. The objects he recovered from its floor, after removing the surface soil, were entirely strange to the local Eskimos, although familiar to some Alaskan natives, who had unearthed many similar specimens in their own country. Since then one discovery has succeeded another, so that today we know that the people among whom I wandered for two years had themselves moved into

Coronation Gulf but a few centuries before, and that their land was once peopled by other tribes of Eskimos who have passed mysteriously from the scene.

Whence came, then, the forefathers of all my Eskimo friends? That question, too, we can now answer with reasonable certainty. Eight or nine hundred years ago, when the Normans were gaining a foothold in England and hardy Icelandic seamen were foundling colonies in the newly discovered "Green Land," numerous tribes of Eskimos roamed the wide expanse of the so-called Barren Lands between Hudson Bay and those two immense expanses of fresh water, Great Bear and Great Slave Lakes. There they hunted caribou and musk-oxen, and in seasons of scarcity trapped and speared fish in the lakes and rivers; but seldom or never did they go down to the sea to hunt the great sea mammals, or to lay in stores of blubber to banish the cold from their huts. Something, then, set these tribes in motion—what, we do not know, unless it was the pressure of Indian tribes pushing up from the southward. The movement gathered force as it proceeded, like a boulder on a hill-side, and the tribes expanded in two directions. Some, going eastward, occupied the shores of Hudson Bay and Baffin Island, and sent a contingent into Greenland; others went northward to the Arctic coast, where another contingent turned west to Coronation Gulf. Gradually the impulse to movement died away; the various tribes settled down in their new homes and lost all memory of their motherland. Only a tell-tale remnant, numbering today about six hundred souls, lingered behind on the Barren Lands, as though it preferred the vicissitudes of the old mode of life, on the old familiar hunting-grounds, to the alluring but often deceitful promises of the new.

# CHAPTER XIII

### THE LAST DAYS

THE harbour ice broke up about the middle of June, and our schooner swayed once more to the gentle motion of the waves. Though the pack in the strait appeared still solid and immovable, a dark line across the sky indicated open water at no great distance, warning us to hasten the preparations for our departure. The house would remain to serve Girling as a mission building, and some of our supplies were hardly worth freighting away; but there were natives to pay for their services, tents and equipment to store deep in the hold, and thousands of specimens, geological, biological, and ethnographic, to label and pack away in boxes, bags, and tins—any receptacle, in fact, that could be made to serve our needs.

Several families of Eskimos that fluctuated between the station and a small fishing-creek four miles away garnered a rich harvest from our packing. They gath-

ered up the empty gasolene cans to convert into cooking-pots, and scrap bars of iron to hammer into chisels
and harpoon shafts. Sometimes they gleaned more
widely than we desired, even carrying away two tarpaulins that covered a cache; but they surrendered
these ill-gotten trophies with great good-humour.
Many offered to help us for a trifling consideration,
such as a half-dozen matches or an old, disused knife;
but there were few tasks that lay within their power.
To distract their attention from more serious matters
we sent them to help Johansen, who was devoting every
spare moment to augmenting his collections of the
various plants and insects. So all one afternoon a
stream of natives flowed steadily toward his tent, call-
ing, "Matches, Johansen, matches," each individual
holding out in payment a fly or a grub sadly crushed
between thumb and forefinger. How many matches
they obtained I cannot say; but since the biological
collections underwent no increase, the experiment was
not continued.

Ikpuck and his family, who were to keep watch over
the station between the time of our departure and
Girling's arrival, pitched their tent beside us for a
short time before joining their countrymen at the fishing-creek. I visited him each day to talk over old
times, and to observe his progress on the new steel
runners that he was fitting to his sled. One evening
Icehouse sent away the children and asked me to lie on

my back with closed eyes, as she wished to interrogate my guardian spirit through the familiar process of head-lifting. She then passed her belt-cord under my head and summoned my spirit to answer her, testing the weight of my head for the answers. Both she and Ikpuck, who sat on the opposite side, appeared very solemn and spoke in hushed tones, so that I could not follow their conversation. Neither could I understand some of the questions she addressed to my "spirit," for she used many expressions confined to songs and religious ceremonies. Yet I realized that she was envisioning the future, when her white son would have gone far away; and she was beseeching my spirit to come to their aid, even from the land of the white man, whenever her family was afflicted with trouble or sickness and called to me for help. "Hearken to our call," she exclaimed again and again; and Ikpuck from his side echoed her entreaty.

We sat in silence after the ceremony, absorbed in our own thoughts. The pathos of their appeal weighed on me heavily. A few short months before I had come out of the mists, a strange and unexpected visitor, to interrupt the peaceful current of their lives. They had received me into their family, nursed me in sickness, clothed me and fed me in times of stress and starvation, bestowed on me the same trust, the same affection, that they gave to their own children. Little it was that I had been able to give them in return. Now they were making their one final appeal. What had my "spirit" answered? What could it answer? When trouble came upon them, as it surely must, and they cried to me for help, would they think me ungrateful if no help came? At last I turned to Icehouse and said, "Sometimes, you know, it is not possible to help." And she answered sadly, "Yes. There are many evil spirits surrounding us, and sometimes no help is possible."

I finished the packing of my specimens before the end of June, and since the heavy ice in the strait would prevent our sailing for at least two weeks, I thought I might travel down to Cape Krusenstern for a farewell view of some Eskimos who were still fishing in the various streams. Patsy was to accompany me, and, with the consent of Ikpuck and Icehouse, I invited Jennie to go with us. She danced with glee at the prospect. Without further delay, we rolled up our packs, loaded two dogs with extra provisions, and marched away over the tundra.

Jennie was the merriest of companions, and the most useful. She laughed when the dogs chased a sandpiper, she laughed when she stumbled over a niggerhead. Her laughter was infectious, and no merrier party ever tramped those northern meadows. She was only twelve years of age, or thirteen at the most, with all a child's love of play and pastime; yet already she knew some of the responsibilities of her sex, and at the end of each day's march insisted on performing all the duties that her mother would have undertaken in the same circumstances. She gathered fuel for our camp-fire while Patsy and I put up the tent, and she super-intended, as far as she knew how, the cooking of the evening meal. Then she dried our marching boots (for we changed to slippers each evening), and, before breakfast, patched any holes that the stones might have cut in their soles the day before. She shot an eider duck along the way with Patsy's rifle, and if we had needed fish would have contrived some means of catch-ing them, where Patsy and I might have failed. Alto-gether, her education was remarkably adapted to the country in which she lived, even though the three R's were not included in the curriculum.

There now befell us an accident, of a kind that in an Arctic winter often leads to serious disaster, but in our circumstances caused only embarrassment. One of our two dogs, prowling with its pack beside a cliff, became wedged in a crevice, and in trying to extricate itself lacerated its foot on a sharp rock. I bandaged the wound with a strip of skin and lightened the ani-mal's load, but it was so crippled that it could hardly keep pace with us. We could not abandon it, nor, if we remained with it, could we hope to reach our destination. To our great relief, however, we found two families of Eskimos camping at the mouth of a small creek, who promised to take charge of the dog for a few days in return for a small butcher-knife.

Shoals of salmon (or, to speak more correctly, salmon-trout), numbering from ten to forty fish in each shoal, had migrated up this stream to spawn in a lake at its source; and a little later in the season young fry, two years old, would migrate from the lake to the sea. The natives captured them by a very simple and effective method. They had built three barriers of stones across the stream, leaving narrow openings in the two that lay nearest the sea and completely closing the highest; whenever a shoal gathered in the upper chamber they blocked its entrance and stabbed the struggling fish with long, three-pointed spears. Nearly a hundred salmon, each weighing from three to twelve pounds, lay spread out on flat boulders around the camp, or hung from horizontal poles; and as many more were cached away under piles of stones. The migration seemed now to have ended, and the two families planned to go inland in search of caribou as soon as they could store away the fish that were still undried.

A larger band of Eskimos who were camped behind Cape Krusenstern had built their weir, not at the mouth of a stream, but in a shallower spot three miles inland near its outlet from a lake. Four and even six shoals of salmon had been ascending each day during the peak of the migration, and a fish that once entered the trap rarely escaped. The shoals then gradually diminished in number, and for two days none at all appeared. The natives, who had nothing to do except deposit their fish in caches as it dried, were lounging around their tents, enjoying the halcyon days of early summer—that week or fortnight, all too brief, when life seemed a glorious holiday. Food was abundant in their camp, and the air so warm that they could sleep in the open air, hardly molested as yet by the clouds of mosquitoes that would shortly darken the sky and attack every living creature, man and beast alike.

Humour is never lacking in an Eskimo community, especially during days of idleness. As the women were gossiping inside a tent, one of the men called out that a shoal had entered the weir. The gathering dispersed in an instant; for although theoretically food was shared in common, the family that gathered the largest store always fared better than the rest, and enjoyed greater prestige. The women, therefore, rushed for their spears and hurried down to the stream. But as they collected on the brink and eagerly scanned the empty water, loud guffaws from the men behind advised them of the hoax, and crestfallen, even amid their laughter, they slowly retreated to their tents again.

About six o'clock the next morning, while the camp still slept, I rose to light our breakfast fire. A woman appeared at the door of her tent, and after gazing tranquilly around, picked up her fish-spear and sauntered down to the weir. As I watched her she shouted, and wading into the water, plied her spear frantically to right and left. Instantly the camp was in an uproar. First the men dashed out, some naked, some half dressed, and, racing headlong to the stream, plunged into the water after her; but all the women loitered in the rear. Then shrieks of laughter mingled with the loud shouts and angry ejaculations of the men; the weir was empty, and the women had taken their revenge.

There was an elderly medicine-man in this camp, one whom we had nicknamed Socrates on account of his snub nose and unusual ugliness. He was a good-natured fellow, but rather dull-witted, and of no great authority among his countrymen because his guardian spirits were credited with little power. He thought fit to hold a séance during our visit, and, from sheer malice, as I believe, directed his utterances against Patsy and myself. Amid much unintelligible nonsense, he alluded to Patsy as the boy whose legs were too long, and to myself as the man who was frightening away the fish by dipping an iron cup into the water, iron, as every one knew, being distasteful to the salmon. But, unfortunately for his credit, the largest shoal of the season unexpectedly entered the weir within two hours of his séance, and the Eskimos, who attributed it to myself in some way, laughed at their seer, who perforce concealed his discomfiture under a foolish smile.

They then offered us several of their finest prizes and entreated us to stay a few days longer, probably hoping for a continuance of their good luck; but I could not linger. We distributed a few needles and matches among them, and departed while their expressions of goodwill still rang in our ears.

This renewal of the salmon migration occurred everywhere along the coast, reaching the two families that were taking care of my dog. Apparently it was an unusual phenomenon, for they, too, ascribed it to my intervention. When I had left them they had shouted after me to "will" that more fish should enter their stream. More fish had come, several shoals of them and they were deeply grateful. So they showered their gratitude on the dog, which was so gorged with fat salmon that it could hardly rise to its feet to welcome us.

The natives who had been camping close to the station had moved away when the first run of the salmon ended, and only Ikpuck and Icehouse remained in possession of their stream. My parents themselves were about to abandon it when the second run started and deluged them with its rapid succession of shoals, four and even five in one day. Husband and wife toiled incessantly for a week, cleaning and drying the fish and storing them away under piles of stones. Never before had they gathered so abundant a supply against the early winter months, when the caribou disappeared to the southward and the ice was too treacherous for the seal-hunt. Yet their joy, great as it was, did not surpass my own, because now I could sail away with the comforting thought that for one year at least starvation would hardly approach their door.

A few days later Cox and I brought them to the station in a large skin boat to which we had attached an outboard motor. They allowed us to pack all their possessions on board without a protest, but drew back in dismay when we suggested their own embarkation. For a long time we urged them in vain, but at last Icehouse yielded, and nervously adjusted herself on the middle thwart. Ikpuck stepped in beside her, he, too, looking somewhat dubious, although he had often speared caribou from a precarious one-man kayak. Seated in the bow facing them, I could not resist the temptation to rock the boat a little. Ikpuck watched me with anxious eyes, but his wife gripped the gunwale desperately with both hands and screamed with all her might. "Jennesi, stop, stop!" she cried as soon as she regained her breath, and added, more quietly, "I did not think my son would ever frighten me so badly." Amazement overcame their fears when we pushed out into deep water and started up the engine; and like happy school-children, they both trailed their hands over the side throughout the journey to feel the swirl of the water.

Another new pleasure awaited them at the station,

for we took them on board the schooner when we made a trial run outside the harbour. It was a genuine voyage of discovery. First they explored the vessel from the forecastle to the stern, peering into every nook and corner except the engine-room, which alarmed them with its fumes and noise. Presently, finding below-decks too prison-like for their fancy, they climbed the stairway again and, standing in the bow, watched with child-like glee the rapid passing of the headlands.

I had promised Ikpuck that I would not leave him unprovided with the weapons and cartridges that he had learned to regard almost as necessities. I had already changed his .44 Winchester for a more powerful 30.30, transferring the former to Jennie; and I now added the .22 automatic rifle on which he had set his heart for killing small game and birds. Two full cases of ammunition went with each new weapon, and for Jennie's .44 I provided brass shells and 3000 primers, with powder and lead to correspond. Of this reloading outfit, however, they promised to reserve one third for The Runner, who had returned to Victoria Island early in May rejoicing in a brand-new .44 and enough ammunition to last him the whole summer.

Other things, too, my family needed, not useless luxuries, but things that would help them in their daily life. Icehouse asked for pots and a frying-pan, needles, thread, scissors, and enough cloth to make several suits of overalls for herself and her household.

Ikpuck received tools of various kinds, a high-powered binocular to aid his hunting, two seines that would supplement his fish-spear and fishing-rod, a light cloth tent to replace the heavy one of skin that he packed all summer on his back, and last, but not least, a Peterborough canoe. Of all these gifts the canoe perhaps pleased him most. We used it immediately to freight most of his dried fish over to a small island that was inaccessible to foxes and other animals until the sea froze over again.

It was melancholy to reflect, during these last days, how little I had done, how little I could do, to ensure the welfare of my family during the years to follow. Nature had not been kind to their land. The winters were long and severe, the summers too short and too late in their arrival to permit the growth of fruits or cereals. Isolated from the great world outside, my parents, like all their tribesmen, could maintain themselves only on what the country itself provided—meat and fish in the spring and summer, fish and meat again in the fall and winter. Permanent homes they had none; life was a perpetual wandering in search of food, a wandering that ended only with death. The winter's twilight had shown me their blurred forms dragging the over burdened sleds from one sealing-ground to another to escape the threat of famine; and the midnight sun had shone on husband, wife, and little daughter, weighted down with heavy packs, stumbling over the trackless land to a new fishing-lake in the hope of breaking their fast before another sleep. Food, clothing, and shelter, those primal necessities that generally come so easily to dwellers in more temperate climes, demanded from them ceaseless effort, until the desperate battle to preserve life seemed almost to nullify any purpose for life. Only an invincibly optimistic race, patient, hardy, and good-tempered, could have wrestled with this environment and survived. What could a white man contribute to its struggle?—a white man who appeared for a season only, then vanished as mysteriously as he came.

The day for our departure arrived at last; the date was July 13, 1916. Heavy ice still lingered outside the harbour, but a channel of open water extended to the westward and widened near the horizon. From morning till nearly evening we laboured at our preparations, striking the last of the tents, dismantling the last of the caches. Everything was finished at 6 o'clock, and, after a hasty supper, I went ashore in the dinghy while my companions pulled up the anchor.

My family had pitched its tent at the entrance to the harbour, where a breeze from the sea blowing across the low promontory kept away the mosquitoes. They were seated outside the doorway, intently watching our movements, but Ikpuck and Jennie came down to the beach to pull up my boat. I sat down beside them, and we watched in silence, Jennie alone in her childish wonder uttering an occasional exclamation. We heard the creaking of the winch as the anchor was lifted, and we saw the vessel swing slowly round and move toward the entrance. Two bells—the engines stopped. "I am going," I said, as I threw at Icehouse's feet the leather belt that I had worn in my wanderings, the belt that she had so often examined with envious eyes. Ikpuck and Jennie pushed off the dinghy. "I am going," I said again, using their only greeting of farewell; and they answered together, "You are going."

In the open channel that led us westward I climbed to the crow's-nest and looked back toward the land through my binoculars. The brown monotonous coast-line rose and fell in gentle undulations far across the moving ice-field. Where shore and ice commingled a solitary tent showed faintly. Something dark beside it seemed to move. Was it Ikpuck?

# L'ENVOI

THE Great War was ended, and I sat at my desk
again, absorbed in the routine of my every-day
work. There was a knock at the door, and
Girling entered, but lately returned from a five years'
sojourn in the land of twilight. "Icehouse sends you
a message," he said; "a message to the son who left
her four years ago. She has heard of your marriage,
and she longs for a picture of the strange white woman
who is now her daughter. She wants, too, a bowl, a
large agate bowl. But the picture she desires more
than all."

Three years passed before the second message came,
this time from Ikpuck. "Jennie your sister is married
and has a son. But I am growing old. Come back and
stay with me once more before I die."

What will the next message say, I wonder? The
country has changed since 1916. Even while we said
our farewells the traders were all heading eastward
to the new land where beautiful white fox skins were
valueless and a fortune could be gained in a night.
White men have invaded it from every quarter, and
the twilight of ignorance and superstition is yielding
to the dawn of a greater knowledge. Bows and arrows
have passed with other weapons into the darkness of

the past, and a new mechanical age has brought magazine rifles, shotguns, steel traps, and even gasolene engines. The caribou are passing with the bows and arrows; of all the herds that once crossed the narrow strait to Victoria Island hardly one now reaches the Arctic shore. Strange diseases are making their appearance, disease that the old-time Eskimo never heard of and for which he has no name. The stern laws of civilization have descended on the land; no longer is infanticide tolerated, or the blood-feud allowed to run its course. "Furs, furs, more furs," is the white man's cry. "Without furs there is no salvation, no ammunition to shoot the scattered game and satisfy your hungry children." The tribal bands where each man toiled for all and shared his food in common are resolving into their constituent families, and every family vies with the rest in the race for wealth and worldly prosperity.

Whither will it all lead? Fifty years ago the cyclone swept over the Eskimos of the Mackenzie River delta, and of its two thousand inhabitants a scant two hundred survive. Fifty years earlier it struck Baffin Island with a similar result. Will history, fifty years hence, record the same fate for this twilight land where for two years we carried on our mission? Were we the harbingers of a brighter dawn, or only messengers of ill-omen, portending disaster?

# EPILOGUE

**F**OUR years after Girling brought me the message from Icehouse a radio station at the mouth of the Coppermine River sent me this call from Ikpuck: "Come back and hunt with me once more on Victoria Island." Jennie added her appeal:

"If you come I will make you a new suit of clothes. But come quickly, for I may not live long."

No call came from Icehouse. She had succumbed a few months earlier to the influenza that had been carried into Coronation Gulf from the white man's world. And Ikpuck never sent a second call.

When summer came round the old hunter wandered back with two or three companions to our stamping grounds on Victoria Island. One morning he went out alone to look for caribou and did not return. No one knows what happened; but of one thing I am sure, that when the angel drew near and offered him the darker draught he drained it without shrinking. Jennie lost her first baby about the same time; and she herself followed it within six months, victim of the tuberculosis that was to carry off her husband also. In America, as elsewhere, the kiss of the white man has brought death to numberless natives whom isolation had protected from our diseases; and the People of the Twilight did not escape.

[ 248 ]

Within ten years of our departure from Bernard Harbour one third of them had been swept away by influenza, and of the hundred Eskimos gathered around the radio station at Coppermine no fewer than twenty-six suffered from advanced tuberculosis.

Was this inevitable? Had we been more conscious of our responsibilities could we have spared them so rude an awakening, so painful an entry into what we call a civilized world? Or does fate spin her web remorselessly, blind to human hopes and weaknesses, indifferent to human suffering?

The children of Jennie's generation who escaped the new diseases underwent a social and economic revolution. Even as we sailed away traders entered their country seeking fox-furs, always fox-furs; and for those pelts so useless for real clothing they offered rifles, shot-guns, steel tools and other goods that promised to make life much easier. So the Eskimos abandoned their communal seal hunts and scattered in isolated families along the coasts in order to trap white foxes during the winter months when the fur of that animal reaches its prime. Their dispersal loosened the old communal ties that had held the families together. The men no longer labored for the entire group, but hunted and trapped each one for his family alone. Their diet and costume changed: more and more it became the diet and costume of the white man. For they had to purchase their winter's supply of food from the trading stores, since trapping left them no time to hunt seals; and they had to buy clothing too from the same stores when the rifles that the traders supplied them exterminated the herds of caribou or drove them into districts far remote. So the new barter economy—furs in exchange for the goods of civilization—made life harder instead of easier, more complicated instead of more simple. The commercial world of the white man had caught the Eskimos in its mesh, destroyed their self-sufficiency and independence, and made them economically its slaves. Only in one respect did it benefit them: it lessened the danger of those unpredictable famines which had overtaken them every ten or fifteen years, bringing suffering and death to young and old without distinction.

Today the youth of the second generation faces another revolution. The atomic age is reaching out towards the Arctic. On this coast and on that stand radar outposts to scan the upper atmosphere, scientific stations to study it and to measure the sun's rays. Already a handful of Jennie's cousins and nephews have found employment at some of these stations: they have unloaded ships and planes, driven motor-boats and caterpillar-tractors, and shown a competence equal to the white man's in operating civilization's simpler machines. Only opportunity and training are lacking to equip them for larger roles. They are adapting themselves, too, to our money economy, and learning to work for a daily wage. But when we who created this money economy ignorantly distort and misapply it, how can we teach Eskimos but one step removed from the stone age to use it for their own and others' welfare, and not for increasing human unhappiness?

DIAMOND JENNESS

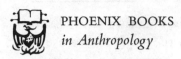 PHOENIX BOOKS
*in Anthropology*

PHOENIX BOOKS
*in Archeology*